God's Presence During Hardship

Daniel and Esther in Exile

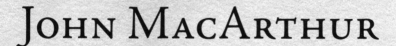

John MacArthur

THOMAS NELSON
Since 1798

NASHVILLE   DALLAS   MEXICO CITY   RIO DE JANEIRO

Published in Nashville, Tennessee, by Thomas Nelson. Thomas Nelson is a trademark of Thomas Nelson, Inc.

Published in association with the literary agency of Wolgemuth & Associates, Inc.

Layout, design, and writing assistance by Gregory C. Benoit Publishing, Old Mystic, CT. ⅁ᴛB

Thomas Nelson, Inc. titles may be purchased in bulk for educational, business, fund-raising, or sales promotional use. For information, please e-mail *SpecialMarkets@ThomasNelson.com*.

ISBN 978-1-4185-3693-0

Printed in the United States of America

09 10 11 12 13 RRD 5 4 3 2 1

CONTENTS

Introduction I

Timeline of Daniel and Esther

Date BC*	Event
605	Nebuchadnezzar takes Daniel captive
603	Daniel interprets Nebuchadnezzar's dream
586	The Babylonians destroy Jerusalem
580	Daniel's friends are kept safe in the fiery furnace
550	Belshazzar assumes the throne in Babylon
539	Babylon falls to Cyrus of Persia
538	The Jews are allowed to return from Persia to Jerusalem
537	Daniel is kept safe in the lions' den
521–486	Darius I reigns in Persia
486–465	Ahasuerus reigns in Persia
483	Ahasuerus holds his banquet
479	Esther goes to Ahasuerus
474	Haman plots against the Jews; Mordecai is honored
458	Ezra leads a group of Jews back to Jerusalem

*Dates are approximate.

INTRODUCTION

In approximately 605 BC, the Lord began to send the people of Judah into captivity in the land of Babylon. One of these was a young man named Daniel who, along with three close friends, found himself serving in the courts of King Nebuchadnezzar. Daniel rose to prominence in Babylon, and lived a long life faithfully serving a succession of kings in two different empires. Years later, around 486 BC, a king named Ahasuerus (also known as Xerxes) came to power in Persia, and he took for his wife a young Jewish woman named Esther.

While the experiences of these two Jews were very different, they shared one thing in common: they faced dangerous situations that threatened their lives because of their faith in God. Through this they each learned the vital lesson that God is sovereign, and He is faithful to those who call upon His name.

In these twelve studies, we will jump back and forth in chronological history, looking at one historical period and then skipping forward or backward in time as needed. We will examine the rise and fall of empires and kings, as well as dreadful dangers faced by God's people. But through it all, we will also learn some precious truths about the character of God, and we will see His great faithfulness in keeping His promises. We will learn, in short, what it means to walk by faith.

✦ WHAT WE'LL BE STUDYING ✦

This study guide is divided into four distinct sections in which we will examine selected Bible passages:

SECTION 1: HISTORY. In this first section, we will focus on the historical setting of our Bible text. These five lessons will give a broad overview of the people, places, and events that are important to this study. They will also provide the background for the next two sections. This is our most purely historical segment, focusing simply on what happened and why.

SECTION 2: CHARACTERS. The four lessons in this section will give us an opportunity to zoom in on the characters from our Scripture passages. Some of these people were introduced in section 1, but in this part of the study guide we will take a much closer look at these personalities. Why did God see fit to include them in His

Book in the first place? What made them unique? What can we learn from their lives? In this practical section, we will answer all of these questions and more, as we learn how to live wisely by emulating the wisdom of those who came before us.

SECTION 3: THEMES. Section 3 consists of two lessons in which we will consider some of the broader themes and doctrines touched on in our selected Scripture passages. This is the guide's most abstract portion, wherein we will ponder specific doctrinal and theological questions that are important to the church today. As we ask what these truths mean to us as Christians, we will also look for practical ways to base our lives upon God's truth.

SECTION 4: SUMMARY. In our final section, we will look back at the principles that we have discovered in the scriptures throughout this study guide. These will be our "takeaway" principles, those which permeate the Bible passages that we have studied. As always, we will be looking for ways to make these truths a part of our everyday lives.

↬ ABOUT THE LESSONS ↫

↬ Each study begins with an introduction that provides the background for the selected Scripture passages.

↬ To assist you in your reading, a section of notes—a miniature Bible commentary of sorts—offers both cultural information and additional insights.

↬ A series of questions is provided to help you dig a bit deeper into the Bible text.

↬ Overriding principles brought to light by the Bible text will be studied in each lesson. These principles summarize a variety of doctrines and practical truths found throughout the Bible.

↬ Finally, additional questions will help you mine the deep riches of God's Word and, most importantly, to apply those truths to your own life.

Section 1:
History

IN THIS SECTION:

～ I ～
CARRIED INTO CAPTIVITY

～ HISTORICAL BACKGROUND ～

From the very foundation of the nation of Israel, God had warned His people that if they turned away from Him and served pagan idols, He would send foreign enemies to destroy their cities and take them captive (Leviticus 26). Nevertheless, the Israelites persisted for generations, running after false gods and indulging in all manner of immoral behavior. The Lord was patient, offering His people many opportunities to repent, but eventually the time came for His discipline. In 722 BC, the Assyrians overran Israel and carried the people into captivity, leaving only the tribe of Judah living around Jerusalem. Judah vacillated between obedience and idolatry for a time, but eventually they, too, were taken into captivity by Babylon.

This captivity actually took place in several stages. The first group to be taken to Babylon included Daniel in 605 BC, and it is at that time that our study opens. When Daniel was taken away, he was a young man, probably around fifteen years old. He found himself in a foreign culture, surrounded by powerful slave-masters who worshiped false gods and ate foods that were forbidden to God's people.

From a human perspective, there would seem to be no hope. A young man, cut off from his people and powerless to resist the forces around him, must certainly compromise his standards or be destroyed. Yet Daniel firmly believed that God was in complete control of his circumstances, and he knew that the Lord would always be faithful to His people—if they would just be faithful to His Word. Daniel, therefore, resolved in his heart to obey God, and the Lord rewarded his obedience with stunning success.

～ READING DANIEL 1:1–21 ～

CARRIED TO BABYLON: *King Nebuchadnezzar's army besieges Judah, as the Lord carries out discipline on His people. Daniel and others are carried into captivity.*

1. THE THIRD YEAR OF THE REIGN OF JEHOIAKIM: That is, 605 BC. Jehoiakim was one of the last kings of Judah.

2. THE LORD GAVE . . . JUDAH INTO HIS HAND: The Lord had warned His people that He would send them into captivity if they did not obey His commands (Leviticus 26), yet the people of Israel (and Judah after the nation of Israel split in two) persisted in idolatry and all manner of disobedience. Israel had been taken into captivity more than a hundred years earlier. Daniel was carried to Babylon during the first wave of captives (probably when he was fifteen years old), although Judah did not finally cease to exist until 586 BC. (For more information, see the previous two books in this series: *A House Divided* and *Losing the Promised Land*.)

SHINAR: That is, Babylon, located in present-day Iraq.

TO THE HOUSE OF HIS GOD: The Babylonians worshiped a number of false gods, notably one called Bel (also known as Marduk or Merodach). King Nebuchadnezzar was effectively making an offering to his false god, thanking him for the victory that (he believed) his god had given him over the God of Judah. Yet, as we will see in both Daniel and Esther, the Lord was not defeated or even faced with a setback; He is absolutely sovereign over the affairs of men and of nations, and this captivity was part of His plan.

BABYLONIAN TRAINING PROGRAM: *The king sets aside a group of gifted young men and grooms them for his special service. Powerful jobs were in the offing, and there was likely much competition.*

4. YOUNG MEN IN WHOM THERE WAS NO BLEMISH: Nebuchadnezzar's stipulation referred primarily to the physical appearance and accomplishments of the young men, but the Old Testament law also called for sacrifices in which there was "no blemish," providing a picture of God's final sacrifice for sins: Jesus Christ, the holy Lamb of God, in whom there was no sin.

WHOM THEY MIGHT TEACH: The Babylonians intended to indoctrinate the young men into the teachings of their culture and pagan religions. Daniel and his friends, however, would prove strong in the Lord, able to assimilate to the fashions and learning of the Babylonians without taking on any of their pagan beliefs.

THE LANGUAGE AND LITERATURE OF THE CHALDEANS: The Chaldeans (or Babylonians) and Assyrians had produced a large body of literature in all genres, much as Great Britain did for modern Western literature. The language commonly spoken in Babylon was Aramaic, which remained a universal tongue in the ancient Middle East until the time of Christ.

5. THE KING'S DELICACIES: These promising young men lived and ate well, literally enjoying the fare of kings. Yet the term *delicacies* in the Old Testament generally carries a negative connotation, indicating self-indulgence in the "finer things" of the world. King Nebuchadnezzar undoubtedly meant to earn the favor and loyalty of these young men, seducing them to abandon their foreign ways and fully embrace Babylonian culture and paganism.

7. NAMES: The act of giving someone a new name demonstrates complete authority over that person, and Nebuchadnezzar was establishing his authority over the young men of Judah. But more than this, the names also indicated that the young men would become subject to the gods of the Babylonians. Their Hebrew names were based upon faith in the Lord: "God is my judge" (Daniel), "Yahweh is gracious" (Hananiah), "Yahweh is my helper" (Azariah), and "Who is like the Lord?" (Mishael). Their new names, however, invoked the names of the false Babylonian gods: Bel, Marduk, and Nebo.

A STEADFAST PURPOSE: *Daniel determines in advance that he will not disobey God's commands, even if it sets him apart from the culture around him—even if he must disobey the king.*

---

8. DANIEL PURPOSED IN HIS HEART: Daniel determined in his heart to be faithful to God even before he was faced with making any decision. The Hebrew might be translated, "he fixed his will" or firmly resolved himself on that course of action.

DEFILE HIMSELF: The king's diet included food that had been sacrificed to idols, as well as things the Lord had commanded His people to not eat (such as pork). To eat such things would have publicly identified Daniel with the false gods, and it would have gone contrary to God's commands. Daniel and his friends were utterly determined that they would not be seduced into pagan practices, even while also being willing to obey the king's will wherever it did not conflict with God's Word. They were striving to be "in the world but not of the world" (John 17:14–16).

9. GOD HAD BROUGHT DANIEL INTO THE FAVOR AND GOODWILL: It is interesting that this verse does not read, "Daniel *found* favor . . . ," but that God specifically *brought* him into favor. Daniel had suffered a tremendous calamity when he was carried forcibly away to Babylon, yet God had not abandoned him. The captivity was part of His deliberate plan, and He was using those who remained faithful to accomplish His purposes. All that was required of Daniel and his friends was that they remain obedient to His Word, and the Lord would take care of the details.

10. I FEAR MY LORD THE KING: We should understand that Daniel also respected King Nebuchadnezzar as the Lord's appointed leader over Babylon, under whose authority

God had placed Daniel and others from Judah. He was, however, in a difficult predicament, wanting to obey the king's edicts while not disobeying God's Word. Yet the Lord was in control, and He would reward Daniel's faithfulness.

Then you would endanger my head before the king: Daniel's request also placed the chief of the eunuchs in a difficult position. He was responsible to carry out King Nebuchadnezzar's plan for grooming these young men for positions of responsibility, and he feared that a change of diet might prove detrimental. But the Lord had given Daniel favor in this man's eyes, and he decided to embrace Daniel's proposal.

12. Please test your servants for ten days: Daniel did not simply go to the steward with a complaint and demand a change of diet; he went with a specific plan in mind that would offer the steward a way out of his dilemma while also enabling Daniel and his friends to obey God's Word. This demonstrated a respect for the king's wishes, while also publicly declaring his obedience to the Lord.

vegetables to eat and water to drink: The Hebrew construction here suggests that the "vegetables" may also have included grain products. The young men chose to drink water rather than the king's wine because it, too, was probably offered to idols prior to being placed upon the table.

13. Then let our appearance be examined: Daniel was fully confident that obedience to God's commands would lead to healthy results. He had no doubt that the Lord would bring the experiment to a successful conclusion.

as you see fit, so deal with your servants: Daniel once again reiterated his willingness to submit to earthly authority. He took pains to make it clear that he wanted to obey both God and the king, and his alternate suggestion was intended merely to remove the conflict.

God Takes Care of the Details: *Daniel's faithfulness to God's Word bears remarkable fruit, as the Lord blesses His servants.*

15. better and fatter in flesh: God gave success to Daniel's proposal, making the four young men healthier and more fit than their peers—and in the brief period of just ten days! This was a remarkably short time for a change of diet to produce visible results, but Daniel's faith and obedience gave God the opportunity to work a miracle for the entire court of Nebuchadnezzar to witness.

17. God gave them knowledge and skill: All gifts and blessings come directly from the hand of God, including even those innate talents and abilities with which we're born. The Lord blessed Daniel and his friends with skill and success in all their endeavors under their captivity; their faithfulness to His commands permitted Him to demonstrate His faithfulness to them.

DANIEL HAD UNDERSTANDING IN ALL VISIONS AND DREAMS: In addition to their intellectual prowess, the Lord also gave Daniel a specific gift for interpretation of visions and dreams. God had a job for Daniel to do, and He provided the skills he'd need to accomplish it.

19. THE KING INTERVIEWED THEM: This was like an important job interview, as the king was examining all the young men to find which were most fit to serve him in demanding official capacities. It is quite likely that there was fierce competition within the ranks of the young men, although the Scripture text does not bring this out, since all would have been vying for the most important positions.

20. HE FOUND THEM TEN TIMES BETTER: It is very significant to remember here that Daniel and his friends did nothing special whatsoever in preparing for their interview with the king—nothing except to steadfastly obey God's commands. It was not their special diet that enabled them to vastly excel over everyone else in the king's service; it was God's blessing of gifts and success. Daniel took care to obey God, and the Lord took care of the rest.

ᨠ FIRST IMPRESSIONS ᨠ

1. Why did God allow the people of Judah to be taken captive by Babylon? If you had been in Daniel's place, how would your slavery have affected your view of God?

2. What was the purpose of Nebuchadnezzar's plan to set apart the young men? What was he preparing them for? What changes did he hope to make in them?

3. Why did Daniel not want to eat the diet of the king? What would the implications have been if he had done so? If you had been in his place, what would you have done?

4. What does it mean that "Daniel purposed in his heart" (v. 8)? How is this done? Why is it important?

↳ Some Key Principles ↶

The Lord may allow hardship, but He is still in control.

The nations of Israel and Judah had persisted in idolatry and disobedience to God's commands, and the time came when He sent discipline upon them. The nation of Israel was carried into captivity by the Assyrians, and years later the people of Judah suffered the same fate at the hands of the Babylonians. The walls of Jerusalem were torn down, the temple was razed, the people's homes were plundered and burned, and those who survived the devastation became prisoners of war and were carried away to a distant land—a land that neither feared God nor knew His Word.

Yet the Lord was still in control over all these circumstances, and He had not abandoned His people. He was sending a time of suffering to the Jews, but that hardship was intended for their purification and strengthening, and it was all part of His plan. Furthermore, it was only for a limited time; at the end of seventy years, God's plan called for some of His people to return and rebuild Jerusalem.

Throughout the course of these studies, we will see repeatedly that God is in complete control over all circumstances in the lives of His people, even at times when life seems to be spiraling out of control. Just as He directed the steps of Daniel and his friends, He will do so in your life as well. As Samuel's mother, Hannah, said, "The LORD kills and makes alive; He brings down to the grave and brings up. The LORD makes poor and makes rich; He brings low and lifts up. He raises the poor from the dust and lifts the beggar from the ash heap, to set them among princes and make them inherit the throne of glory. For the pillars of the earth are the LORD's, and He has set the world upon them. He will guard the feet of His saints" (1 Samuel 2:6–9).

Resolve in your heart to obey God's Word.

Daniel and his three friends were young men when they were carried away by a foreign army, probably in their mid-teens. The temptations and fears they faced can only be imagined, as they found themselves living in a pagan culture with strange gods, traditions, and practices. They were wrenched from home and family, far removed from those who knew and worshiped the true God of Israel. It would have been very easy, therefore, for such young captives to fall into despair, hopelessness, and any number of sinful practices.

But Daniel demonstrated great wisdom when he made a firm resolution in his heart to obey God's commands, whatever might come. He recognized that he was faced with temptations and threats that would lead him into behavior unpleasing to God, and he determined in advance to not be led astray. For him, this meant not eating the food set before him, since it included meats and drink that had been sacrificed to idols and various "unclean" meats—things the Lord had expressly forbidden His people to consume (Exodus 34:13–15; Leviticus 1).

Life is filled with situations that test one's resolve, offering temptations to stray from God's commands as well as pressures to compromise with the world's standards. Fortunately, when we give our lives over to Christ, God gives us His Holy Spirit to empower us to resist and stand firm against those pressures and temptations, but we must still be resolved to act in obedience. The time to make a firm resolution to walk in God's ways is prior to the time of temptation, setting one's heart resolutely to obey the Lord. As Solomon wrote, "Keep your heart with all diligence, for out of it spring the issues of life" (Proverbs 4:23).

Christians must submit to human authorities.

Daniel was in a difficult situation. The Lord had commanded him to abstain from certain types of meat that were considered unclean, and to refrain from eating anything that had been offered as a sacrifice to a pagan idol—yet in Babylon he found himself faced with a steady diet that included both types of forbidden food. What was worse, he had been commanded by the king himself to eat those foods! He seemed forced to choose to either obey God but disobey the king, or follow the king's orders but do what God and the law had commanded to not do.

Yet, in fact, there was a third option. Daniel found a way to submit himself to the king's authority while still obeying God's commands, and the Lord blessed him by giving resounding success to his plan. What underlay Daniel's plan was a genuine respect for the human authorities God had placed him under. His motive was to obey both king and God, not to rebel against human authority under the guise of submitting to the Lord. God commands us to submit to both Him and our earthly authorities, and in most cases it is possible to do both at the same time.

We will see in later studies that this is not absolutely always the case, but even in a very difficult situation Daniel found a way to obey both God and king. This is the Lord's will for all His people, whatever culture or authority they may find themselves under—in society, work, church, and home. In all settings, we are to obey society's laws, follow company policies, and submit ourselves willingly to those whom the Lord has placed in authority. As Paul reminds us, "Let every soul be subject to the governing authorities. For there is no authority except from God, and the authorities that exist are appointed by God. Therefore whoever resists the authority resists the ordinance of God, and those who resist will bring judgment on themselves" (Romans 13:1–2).

∽ DIGGING DEEPER ∽

5. *What part did God play in the events of this chapter? What part did Daniel play? What brought about his stunning success?*

6. *Why did Daniel offer an alternate plan for his diet? Why did he not simply refuse to eat? What might the results have been if he had responded differently?*

7. What evidence did Daniel have that God was in control of his situation? What factors might have tempted him to lose heart? How might you have reacted in his situation?

8. When have you faced a situation where you felt coerced into disobeying God's Word? What did you do? What resulted?

↳ TAKING IT PERSONALLY ↫

9. To what human authorities do you find it difficult to submit? Why? What is your usual response? How might Daniel respond in your circumstances?

10. Is there an area of God's Word in which you are presently compromising with the world's teachings? What will you do this week to change that?

GOD'S PROPHET IN A FOREIGN LAND

∿ HISTORICAL BACKGROUND ∿

Babylon was the most powerful nation in the world in Daniel's day, having already demonstrated its sovereignty over Judah (eventually completely destroying Judah) just as Assyria had done to Israel more than a hundred years earlier. Assyria had been the major world power in that time, as Egypt had been previously. The nations of the world continued to rise and fall, to gain ascendancy only to be overpowered by another, and Babylon would be no exception to that principle.

King Nebuchadnezzar was the most powerful man in the world, yet his great kingdom would not last forever. The Lord made that clear to him one night by sending him a very strange dream, in which he saw a giant statue of a man composed of a variety of metals. Nebuchadnezzar knew that the dream had deep significance, but he could not understand what it meant. But that was not a problem—he had a large group of advisors whom he kept on hand for just such a purpose as this, to interpret prophetic dreams and explain divine mysteries.

These Babylonian advisors were like the scientific and medical experts of our day, specially trained in the vast learning of mankind. They were the most learned men in their fields, claiming to understand the stars, the inner mysteries of man's psyche, and the ways of the gods. Yet Nebuchadnezzar had some doubts about the real extent of their skills, especially when it came to interpreting a prophetic dream. As it turned out, his doubts were well founded.

∿ READING DANIEL 2:1–49 ∿

NEBUCHADNEZZAR'S DREAM: *King Nebuchadnezzar has a troubling dream, and he tests his wise men to find the correct interpretation. The wise men, however, cannot meet his demands.*

1. IN THE SECOND YEAR OF NEBUCHADNEZZAR'S REIGN: Differences in the method of counting a king's years of reign have caused some confusion on exact dates, but this event probably occurred after the three years of Daniel's training were ended, in 603 BC.

HIS SPIRIT WAS SO TROUBLED: This was not the first time God used dreams to warn people of coming events. He used dreams to encourage Joseph (Genesis 37), to warn Pharaoh (Genesis 41), and later we will see how He also used dreams in the life of Esther. King Nebuchadnezzar was troubled because he recognized that his dreams had significance, more than just the idle fancies of sleep, but he was at a loss to understand what they meant.

2. THE MAGICIANS, THE ASTROLOGERS, THE SORCERERS, AND THE CHALDEANS: These men claimed to be "dream experts" who were knowledgeable in medicine and such. The reality is that they practiced the occult arts, including sorcery and astrology— pursuits that God forbids (Deuteronomy 18:10–12). Chaldea was another name for Babylon, but in this usage the word *Chaldeans* refers to men who were learned in the knowledge and literature of the Babylonians.

TO TELL THE KING HIS DREAMS: Notice that the king summoned his experts to tell him what was in his dreams, not merely to interpret them. This demonstrates the uselessness of predicting the future based on interpretations of dreams. Unless there is a prophet with divine revelation from God, there is no way to rightly interpret a dream.

4. TELL YOUR SERVANTS THE DREAM: This certainly seems a natural request; one can hardly be expected to interpret a dream without first being told what the dream was! But Nebuchadnezzar evidently wanted to discover how much his experts really could be relied on in something as important as this.

5. YOU SHALL BE CUT IN PIECES: This judgment may seem unreasonable and harsh at first glance, yet it actually was not entirely unjust. The magicians and astrologers claimed to have insight into the minds of "the gods," thereby claiming that their interpretations were inspired and trustworthy.

7. LET THE KING TELL HIS SERVANTS THE DREAM: The magicians knew that the king was calling their bluff, and they were understandably filled with terror because they knew they could not live up to their false claims of God-given insight.

8. I KNOW FOR CERTAIN THAT YOU WOULD GAIN TIME: The fear and hesitation of the magicians proved to the king that they could not reveal the truth, and now they were just stalling for time.

9. LYING AND CORRUPT WORDS: Those who claim to have special insight into the mind of God often attempt to seduce people through vague words that sound deep and wise, but which contain nothing but corruption. It would be easy enough for the magicians to agree on some abstract interpretation of the dream—if they only knew what it was! Nebuchadnezzar's tactic was both shrewd and wise, as he forced the interpreters to prove their credentials before listening to their interpretation.

11. WHOSE DWELLING IS NOT WITH FLESH: Ironically, this was exactly the point God wanted men of all nations to understand: that He *had* chosen to make His dwelling among them and to make Himself available to them (Isaiah 57:15). He made His presence known through Moses and the nation of Israel, and His plan was ultimately fulfilled through Christ. The Lord now dwells through His Spirit in the lives of His people.

DANIEL PRAYS: *Daniel and his friends find their lives in jeopardy, but they turn to the Lord in prayer. God grants their requests and gives Daniel the wisdom to answer the king.*

13. THEY SOUGHT DANIEL AND HIS COMPANIONS: Evidently the king's special training for the young men was to groom them for such counsel as was presently called for. The abysmal failure of the magicians put Daniel's life in danger, as he was considered one of them.

14. WITH COUNSEL AND WISDOM DANIEL ANSWERED ARIOCH: Once again we find Daniel approaching human authority figures with deference and wisdom. It is possible that he'd heard about the king's decree and had time to seek wise counsel with his three godly friends. It is quite certain, however, that the Lord was with him and gave him wisdom, even if he was caught unawares by this sudden summons.

16. ASKED THE KING TO GIVE HIM TIME: Once again, Daniel offered an alternative plan to the king, as he had done concerning the diet in chapter 1.

18. SEEK MERCIES FROM THE GOD OF HEAVEN: Daniel and his friends knew exactly what to do in this crisis: pray! The Lord had given Daniel a gift of understanding dreams (1:17), yet he clearly recognized that his gift lay in God's hands, not in himself. He trusted that the Lord would be faithful to reveal the dream to him, but he also understood that the Lord wants His people to turn to Him in prayer, asking Him to remember His promises.

21. HE CHANGES THE TIMES AND THE SEASONS: Daniel's prayer of worship addresses a very important aspect of God's character: His sovereignty. God is absolutely in control of all earthly affairs, including raising kings and deposing them and extending to the very changes of the seasons.

27. THE SOOTHSAYERS CANNOT DECLARE TO THE KING: Nebuchadnezzar's demands were impossible for any man to fulfill, as only God can fathom the heart of a man and reveal his innermost thoughts. Nebuchadnezzar undoubtedly recognized this, and was looking for a man who had a special relationship with God (or with "the gods," as he likely would have understood it).

THE DREAM: *Daniel first describes the king's dream, then gives him the interpretation from God. The final fulfillment will come in the future when Christ returns.*

31. A GREAT IMAGE: That is, a huge statue of a man. The statue was composed of various metals, as listed in the following verses.

32–33. GOLD . . . SILVER . . . BRONZE . . . IRON . . . CLAY: The list of metals gradually decreased in value while increasing in strength. Gold, silver, and bronze were all used decoratively for their shining beauty, while bronze was used in weaponry until it was superseded by the stronger (but unattractive) iron. Yet even though the metals increased in strength, they culminated in a mixture of iron and clay, which would be the weakest item in the list. Indeed, iron weakened by clay would have no practical purpose at all, either for weaponry or decoration.

34. A STONE WAS CUT OUT WITHOUT HANDS: That is, no hands were used in cutting out the stone. This is an image of Christ, also referred to as *"a stumbling stone and rock of offense"* (Romans 9:33).

35. NO TRACE OF THEM WAS FOUND: The statue of various metals represented the many human kingdoms that have risen and fallen throughout the history of mankind. When Christ finally sets up His millennial kingdom, every governmental system mankind has ever established will be of no account; it will be as though none had ever existed.

37. THE GOD OF HEAVEN HAS GIVEN YOU A KINGDOM, POWER, STRENGTH, AND GLORY: The statue's golden head represented Nebuchadnezzar and the great kingdom of Babylon. According to Daniel's words, there has never been another kingdom as majestic and glorious on the earth. Yet even in giving this grand praise to the king, Daniel made it clear that his great accomplishments were entirely given to him from the hand of God; there was no room for Nebuchadnezzar to take credit or pride in his kingdom.

39. BUT AFTER YOU SHALL ARISE ANOTHER KINGDOM: As grand and majestic as Babylon was, it was still only an earthly, human system of government, and as such its days were numbered. No human government will ever last; only the government established by the King of kings and Lord of lords will endure.

40. THE FOURTH KINGDOM SHALL BE AS STRONG AS IRON: The nations represented in the dream were: Babylon (gold); Medo-Persia (silver); Greece (bronze); Rome (iron); a future earthly domain (iron and clay). The Roman Empire was indeed as powerful as iron; its ironclad armies were known as the Iron Legions of Rome. The Roman Empire was known for its ruthless ability to crush any nation that resisted its authority.

42. PARTLY OF IRON AND PARTLY OF CLAY: This picture does in some measure describe the last days of the Roman Empire, when Rome grew unable to control its far-flung dominions. But the complete fulfillment of this dream has yet to take place, as Daniel's further interpretation makes clear. Most scholars view the feet as representing a future revival of the Roman Empire, or some human government set up in its style that will rule all or most of the world. The toes are probably the ten kings described in Daniel's later vision (Daniel 7), representing ten rulers who will form a confederation in the future. This kingdom will be both powerful and weak, and will be the existing world power at the time of Christ's return.

43. THE SEED OF MEN: This verse seems to suggest that the final kingdom will be a heterogeneous mixture of many nations who will not remain loyal to one another, when push comes to shove. But the phrase "the seed of men" reminds us that, whatever form a human government may take, it is still a product of the schemes of men, and as such it cannot endure.

44. A KINGDOM WHICH SHALL NEVER BE DESTROYED: This will be the millennial kingdom, established by Christ at His second advent. It will continue on earth for a thousand years (a millennium), after which will come the final judgment and His eternal heavenly kingdom (Revelation 20). God will establish His kingdom, ruled by His Son, and it will endure throughout all eternity without interruption. It will not be superseded by "another people," as was the case with each of the nations in the dream, but will instead crush and obliterate all forms of human government that have been attempted throughout the history of the world.

45. THE STONE WAS CUT OUT OF THE MOUNTAIN WITHOUT HANDS: This is a reference to Christ, who is both fully man and fully God. He was born of a virgin, not from the seed of man, and His nature took human form by the direct intervention of God.

THE DREAM IS CERTAIN: Nebuchadnezzar's dream was a prophecy sent from God, and as such its fulfillment was—and is—absolutely certain. Most of it, in fact, has already come to pass, and indeed is ancient history to us today, as the empires of Persia, Greece, and Rome have long since faded away. But the vision of God's future kingdom under His Son will absolutely come to pass, and nothing can prevent its fulfillment.

46. Nebuchadnezzar fell on his face, prostrate before Daniel: Daniel had indeed accomplished what no human could do: he had described the king's dream as well as interpreted its meaning. Nebuchadnezzar recognized that no human agency could have accomplished this miracle, and this offering was presumably intended for the Lord, not for Daniel (who would have instantly refused it otherwise).

47. Truly your God is the God of gods: Daniel's faithfulness made it clear that the king's dream had been interpreted correctly only through the power of God, and as a result the king himself publicly acknowledged that the Lord is the King of kings. There are no other gods before Him.

48. he made him ruler over the whole province of Babylon: The Lord had used Joseph in a very similar manner in Egypt more than a thousand years earlier (Genesis 41), and in both cases His plan was for the greater good of His people. God holds complete control over all events of our personal lives, but His plan extends to all people throughout time and into eternity.

ᨓ First Impressions ᨓ

1. *Why did King Nebuchadnezzar insist that his wise men describe his dream? What did this reveal about his expectations concerning its interpretation?*

2. *Why were the wise men unable to describe the dream? What did this reveal about the source of their powers?*

3. *How did Daniel respond when asked to go before the king? What did this reveal about his character?*

4. *What did the dream represent? What characteristics were revealed about the various kingdoms? About the final kingdom?*

⌁ Some Key Principles ⌁

Jesus will one day return to earth and establish His eternal kingdom.

Nebuchadnezzar's strange dream pictured a succession of world powers, beginning with his own reign over Babylon and stretching out more than five hundred years through the age of the Roman Empire. Those world powers formed the body of the statue in the king's dream, from the golden head of Babylon down through the iron legs of Rome, and each of those nations has long since faded into ancient history. Yet one part of that dream has yet to be fulfilled: the feet of clay, smashed by a rock hurled from heaven.

That rock is Jesus, and the statue's feet represent a world kingdom that is yet to be established. At some future date, Christ will return and take control over all the earth, abolishing all forms of human government and establishing His throne over all peoples and dominions. He will take up His scepter as King of kings and Lord of lords, and all the nations of earth will bow before Him. He will maintain this earthly kingdom for a thousand years (called the Millennium), after which He will bring about a new heaven and a new earth (Revelation 20–21).

As Daniel told Nebuchadnezzar, these events are certain and sure. As truly as the dream was fulfilled concerning the kingdoms of the past, so it shall also be fulfilled concerning the events of the future. Those who acknowledge Him now as Lord of their lives will be resurrected to rule with Him in His eternal kingdom—but those who refuse His gift of salvation will rise again in the final resurrection and face His judgment of eternal condemnation. The time of salvation is now, as Scripture warns us. "We then, as workers together with Him also plead with you not to receive the grace of God in vain. For He says: 'In an acceptable time I have heard you, and in the day of salvation I have helped you.' Behold, now is the accepted time; behold, now is the day of salvation" (2 Corinthians 6:1–2).

The wisdom of this world cannot explain the truths of God.

King Nebuchadnezzar had a dream that he could not understand. Ordinarily, he would have turned to his magicians and counselors for an explanation, but on this occasion he shrewdly realized that the wise men of his age might try to cover their ignorance by inventing an interpretation that would be difficult to prove or disprove—so he demanded that his counselors begin their interpretation by first describing the dream itself. And this, of course, would be impossible for any man to accomplish.

But the dream had been sent not by human agencies but by God, and it was an easy matter for God to tell Nebuchadnezzar both the dream and its interpretation. It is significant that He chose to do this not through the great learning of men but through His obedient servant Daniel. The wisdom of mankind cannot comprehend the mind of God. The world prides itself on our great learning and advances in the fields of science, medicine, physics, biology, and so forth, but no field of human study or endeavor can reveal the eternal truths of God.

Only God can reveal Himself to mankind, and He has chosen to do so through His Word and His Son. The Bible encapsulates the truth of God in written form, but Jesus Christ embodied the person of God in human form. To know Jesus is to know the mind of God. On the other hand placing one's faith in modern science and man's intellect is like Nebuchadnezzar trusting in his wise men. As Paul wrote, "Let no one deceive himself. If anyone among you seems to be wise in this age, let him become a fool that he may become wise. For the wisdom of this world is foolishness with God. For it is written, 'He catches the wise in their own craftiness'; and again, 'the Lord knows the thoughts of the wise, that they are futile'" (1 Corinthians 3:18–20).

God reveals Himself to those who seek Him.

Nebuchadnezzar's astrologers and magicians were filled with terror when the king commanded them to describe his dream, for they recognized that no human could ever accomplish such a thing. "There is no other who can tell it to the king except the gods," they cried, "whose dwelling is not with flesh" (Daniel 2:11). They did not trust the Lord, and so of course they did not turn to God for guidance.

Daniel knew that the magicians were partly right: the correct interpretation was only available from God (not "the gods" whom the magicians served); but he also knew that they were partly wrong: Daniel sought the Lord in prayer, and knew that God would guide him through this trial. Daniel had no way of knowing that the Lord would indeed reveal the dream to him, but he and his friends knew that their only hope was to trust God, who was in control of the situation. As a practical point of consideration, it is helpful for us to think about how God also reveals himself to people today. As stated in the previous principle, God cannot be known by any means except a saving faith in His Son, Jesus Christ. Paul explained this truth to the wise men of his day: "God, who made the world and everything in it, since He is Lord of heaven and earth, does not dwell in temples made with hands. Nor is He worshiped with men's hands, as though He needed anything, since He gives to all life, breath, and all things. And He has made from one blood every nation of men to dwell on all the face of the earth, and has determined their preappointed times and the boundaries of their dwellings, so that they should seek the Lord, in the hope that they might grope for Him and find Him, though He is not far from each one of us; for in Him we live and move and have our being" (Acts 17:24–28).

⌁ DIGGING DEEPER ⌁

5. *Why was Christ pictured as a rock "cut out of the mountain without hands" (v. 45)? Why did His kingdom smash the statue to dust?*

6. *What "experts" would likely be called to interpret such a dream today? How would they fare?*

7. Why did God reserve the interpretation of the dream for Daniel? Why did He not reveal it to the magicians and astrologers? to King Nebuchadnezzar?

8. What is revealed about the character of God in this chapter? List below some of His attributes; then spend time in worship.

⌁ Taking It Personally ⌁

9. In response to the future kingdom in which Jesus Christ will reign, have you thought seriously about where you stand before God? Have you considered the implications if you refuse to acknowledge Christ as your Savior and King? If not, what is preventing you right now? If you don't accept Christ as Savior and King, how does this affect your involvement in His coming kingdom?

10. When confronted with a difficult situation, do you generally turn first to the wisdom of the world, or to God's Word? What would Daniel do in a similar situation?

~ 3 ~
HANDWRITING ON THE WALL

DANIEL 5

⌁ HISTORICAL BACKGROUND ⌁

King Nebuchadnezzar died around 562 BC after ruling in Babylon for forty-two years. His son Evil-Merodach (meaning "servant of Merodach," a pagan god) took up his throne, but kept it for only two years. He was murdered by his sister's husband, who took the throne for another brief reign and was succeeded by his own son. This king was overthrown by a revolution in 556 BC, a mere six years after the end of Nebuchadnezzar's powerful reign, and one of the conspirators, named Nabonidus, ascended the throne.

Nabonidus eventually installed his son Belshazzar on the throne of Babylon as co-regent while he traveled throughout the empire, trying to bolster its weakening authority. His efforts proved futile, however, as the empire of the Medes and Persians was growing ever more powerful under the leadership of Cyrus the Great. In 539 BC, the Persian army besieged the Babylonian capital, ending the Babylonian Empire in one abrupt military venture.

This chapter of Daniel takes place on that very night in 539 BC, in the palace of Belshazzar, who was willfully choosing to ignore the Persian army that had gathered outside his city gates. On that fateful night, Belshazzar committed acts of blasphemy against God, and the Lord responded by sending a very dramatic message.

⌁ READING DANIEL 5:1–31 ⌁

HANDWRITING ON THE WALL: *Belshazzar has become king in Babylon, but his attitude is very different from Nebuchadnezzar's. One night he holds a great feast and blasphemes God.*

1. **BELSHAZZAR THE KING:** Belshazzar (meaning "Bel protect the king") was actually a co-regent with his father, Nabonidus, who had acceded to the throne of Babylon after a revolution overthrew the descendants of Nebuchadnezzar. The events

in this chapter occurred around 539 BC, roughly sixty-five years after Nebuchadnezzar's dream (Study 2).

THE KING MADE A GREAT FEAST: The Medo-Persian army was holding the city under siege, and Belshazzar evidently decided to drown his sorrows in an orgy. It was to be his last deed as ruler of Babylon, and the last night of his life.

2. THE GOLD AND SILVER VESSELS: These were the sacred vessels from the temple in Jerusalem, which Nebuchadnezzar's army had plundered when Daniel was taken captive. This was a blasphemous act, using the sacred vessels from God's temple at a profane, drunken orgy.

4. PRAISED THE GODS OF GOLD AND SILVER, BRONZE AND IRON, WOOD AND STONE: To add to their defiance of God, the revelers used the sacred vessels to sing praises to false gods.

5. THE FINGERS OF A MAN'S HAND APPEARED: Babylonian hands had taken the sacred vessels from God's temple and had raised those vessels in praise to false gods; now the hand of God appeared to respond to their defiance.

6. HIS KNEES KNOCKED AGAINST EACH OTHER: This would be an almost comical picture of a man stricken helpless with fear, if not for the deeply serious nature of the king's defiance against God. Yet Belshazzar's attitude toward the things of God suggests he might have simply ignored a less-dramatic method of learning God's message.

7. THE ASTROLOGERS, THE CHALDEANS, AND THE SOOTHSAYERS: Belshazzar responded to his crisis just as Nebuchadnezzar had done, calling upon the secular "experts." Turning to the wisdom and understanding of men for an explanation is the normal response of the world when confronted with something miraculous. As we saw in Study 2, however, the wisdom of the world cannot comprehend the things of God.

THE THIRD RULER IN THE KINGDOM: Belshazzar's father was actually the king, and Belshazzar was co-regent, making him the second in command. Purple robes and golden chains were adornments of kings. The sad irony was that the kingdom was about to collapse; such an offer of power would last for a matter of hours, and was utterly meaningless.

INTERPRETING THE WRITING: *The king's wise men cannot interpret the meaning of the writing on the wall. Fortunately, the Queen Mother remembers Daniel.*

8. THEY COULD NOT READ THE WRITING: Belshazzar had not learned from the experiences of Nebuchadnezzar, and thus was doomed to repeat the lesson.

10. The queen: Probably the Queen Mother, since Belshazzar's wives and concubines were already present.

11. There is a man in your kingdom: It is hard to believe that Daniel had been forgotten by this new king, especially since Nebuchadnezzar had elevated him to such an important position. The life of Joseph bears striking similarities to that of Daniel, including being elevated to the right hand of Pharaoh—and subsequently completely forgotten by those who came after (Exodus 1:8).

in whom is the Spirit of the Holy God: It is significant that the one thing people remembered about Daniel was that he was indwelt by the Spirit of God. The queen also publicly acknowledged that Daniel's God was the one true, holy God, quite distinct from the false gods being praised by the drunken king.

your father: This was probably a figurative use of the title, as Belshazzar appears to not have been related to Nebuchadnezzar. The fact that the queen repeated this twice more suggests that she was either trying to flatter the king or, quite possibly, trying to alert him to the trust that Nebuchadnezzar had placed in Daniel. She may well have been alarmed at the terrible disparity between the leadership of Nebuchadnezzar and the drunken incompetence of Belshazzar.

12. an excellent spirit: This might refer to Daniel's attitude of willingness to serve, or it might simply mean that he had a high aptitude for such puzzles. But the unintended meaning is the most accurate: Daniel did indeed have an excellent Spirit directing him, the Spirit of God.

13. one of the captives from Judah: This suggests that the successors to Nebuchadnezzar had forgotten Daniel's high position and value. He was once again viewed as merely a slave, captured in time of war.

Daniel's Interpretation: *Daniel reminds the king of his predecessor's lesson in humility; then he interprets God's message. It is not good news for Belshazzar.*

17. give your rewards to another: Daniel's blunt response was intended not to be rude, but to make it clear that he would interpret the writing out of obedience to the Lord and to the king, not because of any promised reward. He might also have recognized how worthless those gifts would become, since Belshazzar's kingdom was at an end.

18. God gave Nebuchadnezzar: Daniel began his explanation by reminding Belshazzar that his present authority was only by God's hand. What God had given, He could also take away.

19. WHOMEVER HE WISHED: The numerous repetitions of this phrase underscored the fact that Nebuchadnezzar had grown proud under the tremendous blessings God had bestowed on him, forgetting where his power came from and taking the credit to himself.

21. HIS HEART WAS MADE LIKE THE BEASTS: Nebuchadnezzar had gone mad for a time and went about eating grass like an ox. We will read more about this in Study 7.

THE MOST HIGH GOD RULES IN THE KINGDOM OF MEN: Nebuchadnezzar had learned the vital lesson that God is absolutely sovereign over all the affairs of men, and that kings and kingdoms rise and fall according to His will—and not otherwise.

22. ALTHOUGH YOU KNEW ALL THIS: Belshazzar knew the history of King Nebuchadnezzar, including the important lessons he'd learned concerning the sovereignty of God—yet he had stubbornly refused to humble himself. He had evidently ignored God's earlier warnings, so now the Lord had used a method he could not ignore, causing a mysterious hand to appear and write the message on the very walls of his palace.

23. YOU HAVE PRAISED THE GODS: Belshazzar went beyond refusing to humble himself before God by committing an open act of defiance against Him: using the sacred vessels to honor false gods, worshiping created things rather than the Creator. By doing so, he defied the God who had created him and placed him in authority over Babylon, and that same God was about to take back what He had given.

25. MENE, MENE: Each of these words was a unit of measurement, but the phrase translates to mean "numbered, numbered, weighed, divided," as Daniel's interpretation showed. The Lord had weighed Belshazzar's spirit and found it wanting in humility before Him.

↶ FIRST IMPRESSIONS ↷

1. *Why would King Belshazzar throw a great feast when the Persian army was surrounding the city? What does this reveal about his kingship?*

2. *Why did Belshazzar use the sacred vessels from God's temple? What did this act reveal about his attitude toward God?*

3. What reasons might God have had to send His message via a mysterious hand writing on the wall? Why not just have a prophet deliver the message?

4. What did God's message mean to Belshazzar? What was Belshazzar's response? What did his response reveal about the state of his heart before God?

↵ Some Key Principles ↵

God gives His people the words to speak at the right time.

Daniel found himself in numerous difficult situations, as we have already seen. He was called before several kings to interpret messages from God that no one else in the kingdom could comprehend—and at times his life was on the line. The Lord had given him the gift of interpreting dreams and prophecies, yet he made it abundantly clear that such interpretations were given to him directly from God; they were not the result of his own strength, wisdom, or abilities. And God was faithful in each instance to give Daniel the words he was to speak.

It's important to recognize, however, that Daniel did not know what he would say until the time came for him to speak. He did not know what words were written on the wall in Belshazzar's banquet hall until he got there, and he did not even know the content of Nebuchadnezzar's dream until the Lord revealed it to him. We can easily imagine how unnerving it must have been to have no idea what to say to a king demanding an interpretation where all others have failed. Yet this was precisely what the Lord called His servant to do, forcing Daniel to trust in God's faithfulness and sovereignty, and making it clear to the king and his court that the words were from Him.

This does not mean a Christian should be lazy and haphazard in the work the Lord calls him to do. Peter, for instance, urged his readers to "always be ready to give a defense to everyone who asks you a reason for the hope that is in you" (1 Peter 3:15). But Jesus also warned His disciples that they would sometimes "be brought before governors and kings" to give testimony to the gospel. At such times, the Lord said, "do not worry about how or what you should speak. For it will be given to you in that hour what you should speak; for it is not you who speak, but the Spirit of your Father who speaks in you" (Matthew 10:18–20). "I will give you a mouth and wisdom which all your adversaries will not be able to contradict or resist" (Luke 21:14–15). These verses are not an excuse for laziness but rather a comfort during persecution.

Just as God was faithful to give Daniel the right words at the right time, He will do the same for you. We can have confidence that God will enable us to be a faithful witness no matter the situation in which we find ourselves.

Worship the Creator, not His creation.

King Belshazzar threw a drunken party for his friends and courtiers, and in their licentious frenzy they ate and drank from sacred vessels that had been dedicated to the Lord's temple in Jerusalem. This blasphemous act demonstrated an utter contempt for the God of Israel, but the revelers took their blasphemy one step further: they openly praised and worshiped fictitious "gods of silver and gold, bronze and iron, wood and stone" (v. 23). In doing so, they worshiped the creation rather than the Creator.

Such paganism is still practiced today, and is in fact becoming very widespread in Western nations. Under the guise of "environmentalism," for example, many today deny that God created the earth and mankind, while simultaneously elevating His creation in His place. It is a bitter irony to treat the things of God with disdain, as Belshazzar did, while praising the very things He made.

The Bible warns that this idolatrous attitude inevitably leads to the downfall of a nation, just as it did in Babylon during the time of King Belshazzar. Paul wrote that the wonders of creation are intended to teach men about God, not to replace Him as their Lord. When a nation replaces the Creator with the creation, however, all forms of wickedness inevitably follow. "Professing to be wise," Paul warned, "they became fools, and changed the glory of the incorruptible God into an image made like corruptible man—and birds and four-footed animals and creeping things. Therefore God also gave them up to uncleanness, in the lusts of their hearts, to dishonor their bodies among themselves, who exchanged the truth of God for the lie, and worshiped and served the creature rather than the Creator, who is blessed forever" (Romans 1:22–25).

All earthly authority comes directly from God.

King Belshazzar ruled over one of the world's wealthiest and most powerful nations. Babylon was in decline under his leadership, yet his heart was filled with pride and self-congratulation, taking the credit to himself for the power he wielded. His predecessor Nebuchadnezzar had faced the same lesson, but he had learned what Belshazzar rejected: that all authority is given by God, who can take it away as easily as He gives it.

Daniel tried to explain this principle to Belshazzar, stating emphatically that "the Most High God gave Nebuchadnezzar your father a kingdom and majesty, glory and honor" (v. 18). But the truth was that Belshazzar already knew these things, yet he persistently refused to humble himself before Almighty God. Indeed, as we have seen, his stubborn pride led him to openly defy God's authority, and in the end both his kingly authority and his very life came to an abrupt end.

Most of us will never become kings or queens, yet we all interact with earthly authority throughout our lives. We exercise authority in the home or workplace, and we are simultaneously called to submit to others who are in authority over us. Recognizing that God is the source of all authority helps us remain humble in exercising what authority we have been given. It also enables us to submit willingly, even when doing so seems unpleasant.

∿ Digging Deeper ∿

5. What does it mean that Belshazzar and his guests "praised the gods of gold and silver, bronze and iron, wood and stone" (v. 4)? How is this done in the world today?

6. How did Daniel know the meaning of the mysterious message on Belshazzar's wall? What principle does this illustrate?

7. In what ways did Belshazzar fail to learn from the experiences of Nebuchadnezzar? What lessons might he have learned? How might his life have been different?

8. How did the Queen Mother (v. 10) differ from Belshazzar? Why did she keep mentioning "your father the king" (referring to Nebuchadnezzar)?

⌁ Taking It Personally ⌁

9. How do you respond to authority? How do you handle the areas of authority that you've been given? How does this chapter reflect on both areas of authority?

10. When have you faced a situation where you didn't know what to say? How did the Lord give you wisdom and guidance in that situation?

~ 4 ~
GOD'S CHOSEN QUEEN

∽ HISTORICAL BACKGROUND ∽

We now move forward in time to some sixty years after the fall of Babylon, which we considered in the last study. Our story changes from the courts of Babylon to the courts of Persia. We will meet the great King Xerxes (also called Ahasuerus) at his palace in the capital city of Susa. At this point in history, some Jews had returned to Jerusalem and started rebuilding the temple (events covered in the next book in this series, *Rebuilding God's City*), but many were still living in exile.

We will meet two such people in this study: a young woman named Esther and her adopted father Mordecai. They were living in a foreign land and were sometimes faced with anti-Semitism and persecution. That anti-Semitism was about to reach a peak of dreadful persecution, and God's people were about to be threatened with annihilation. This threat would catch the Jews by surprise, but not God; He had a plan already in place, and we will see how He worked it out to protect His people from their enemies. This study opens in 479 BC, and the events unfold over a period of approximately six years.

∽ READING ESTHER 2:1–18 ∽

ROYAL JOB OPENING: *The king of Persia has deposed his queen because she disobeyed his commands. Now it's time to find a new queen, and the king holds a national competition of suitable candidates.*

1. AFTER THESE THINGS: The events in this passage took place in Persia in approximately 479 BC, some sixty years or so after the events covered in Study 3.

WHEN THE WRATH OF KING AHASUERUS SUBSIDED: The king had given a great feast, during which he had sent for his wife, Queen Vashti, to come before him—and she had refused. He responded by decreeing that Vashti could never again enter his presence. Ahasuerus is more commonly known to us today as Xerxes.

2. Let beautiful young virgins be sought for the king: Kings in this culture had the right to claim a young woman as an addition to his harem, which amounted to a collection of concubines. It was customary for such women to undergo a full year of special beauty treatments, training, and purification rites prior to becoming part of the king's harem. They enjoyed courtly privileges and status, and were housed separately from the rest of the king's household.

5. the son of Kish, a Benjamite: It appears that Esther's cousin Mordecai was descended directly from Kish, the father of King Saul, of the tribe of Benjamin. This small fact will become extremely significant in the conflict with Haman, as we'll see in a later study.

Enter Esther: *One of the candidates chosen for the king's harem is a young Jewish woman named Esther. She didn't know it at the time, but the Lord had important plans for her life.*

8. Esther also was taken to the king's palace: We are not told Esther's views on the matter, but they would have been irrelevant anyway. She went because the king commanded it, whether she liked the arrangement or not. On the surface this might have been seen as a very bad situation by Esther and Mordecai, but the Lord's hand was guiding, and this was part of His sovereign plan.

9. the young woman pleased him: Here we begin to see the Lord's invisible hand of guidance in the affairs of Esther and the Jews. The Lord granted her favor in the eyes of Hegai, the king's chief eunuch, who was responsible for selecting the "finalists" in the selection of the next queen, just as He had given Daniel favor in the eyes of Nebuchadnezzar. God is never mentioned in the book of Esther, but the author leaves it to the reader to discern the ways in which the Lord controlled the events. At the same time, Esther would not have obtained favor from Hegai if she'd exhibited an unwilling or resentful attitude toward her situation. She, like Daniel, trusted that the Lord was in control and submitted herself under His hand.

10. Esther had not revealed her people or family: Here we have the first glimmer of foreshadowing, suggesting that there was some strong anti-Semitic sentiment in the city that led Mordecai to feel safer if Esther's Jewish heritage were not known.

11. Mordecai paced in front of the court: The women's quarters would have been absolutely forbidden to any male visitor except the king and his chosen eunuchs, so Mordecai would have been unable to make direct contact with Esther. Jewish tradition holds that he was an official of some small capacity in the king's court, although later events suggest he may have held a position of some importance. Regardless, his constant concern for his cousin's safety and welfare was amply demonstrated by the fact that he made himself available to receive news on a daily basis.

15. SHE REQUESTED NOTHING: Esther demonstrated wisdom as well as a submissive spirit. We will look more closely at her character in Study 8.

17. THE KING LOVED ESTHER: The world would see this as mere chance, the function of the human heart alone, but in reality the Lord was fully in control. It was He who bestowed the king's favor and grace upon Esther, and it was He who removed Queen Vashti and set Esther in her place. "The king's heart is in the hand of the LORD, like the rivers of water; He turns it wherever He wishes" (Proverbs 21:1).

⤳ READING ESTHER 4:5–17 ⤫

UNCOVERING A DEADLY PLOT: *A man named Haman holds a strong hatred for the Jews, and he has cooked up a plot to destroy them all. But God has another plan in mind.*

5. WHAT AND WHY: Esther sent one of the king's eunuchs to find out why Mordecai was going about in open mourning and loud lamenting about the city. The reason was that a man named Haman had persuaded the king to make an edict to annihilate the entire Jewish population of Persia, as Queen Esther would quickly learn.

7. THE SUM OF MONEY: Haman had offered the king a huge sum of money for the privilege of exterminating the Jews, amounting to approximately two-thirds of the empire's annual budget! The fact that Mordecai knew such details might indicate that he held a position of influence at the court, or it might merely demonstrate how much talk was generated by Haman's stunning plan.

8. SHOW IT TO ESTHER AND EXPLAIN IT TO HER: Evidently Esther had not yet heard about Haman's wicked scheme, as the king evidently shielded his queen and his entire harem very carefully from any outside influences.

THAT HE MIGHT COMMAND HER: It seems surprising that Mordecai took it for granted that he could command the queen, yet it also demonstrates the humble spirit that Esther maintained, even in her exalted situation. She was queen over the most powerful nation on earth, yet she was still open to her cousin's guidance.

11. PUT ALL TO DEATH: Even though Esther was the queen, she was not exempt from the king's law that anyone entering his presence without an invitation would be put to death. Mordecai had asked Esther to risk her very life for her people.

13. DO NOT THINK . . . THAT YOU WILL ESCAPE: Esther had not revealed the fact that she was a Jew, and it is possible that she thought she could escape detection. If she did entertain such a notion at all, however, she quickly abandoned it.

14. RELIEF AND DELIVERANCE WILL ARISE FOR THE JEWS: Mordecai demonstrated the depth of his faith in God, declaring confidently that the Lord would find a way to deliver His people from destruction—with or without the cooperation of the queen.

FOR SUCH A TIME AS THIS: Mordecai also recognized that God's sovereignty extended to all affairs of their lives, including whatever situations they found themselves in. He saw that the Lord had indeed placed Esther on the throne of Persia so that she might be involved in His plan to protect His people. The flip side to this principle, however, is that Esther had to choose to obey if she were to fulfill the Lord's purpose in her own life.

16. FAST FOR ME: Esther did not pretend her task was easy; she knew it was beyond her own power to succeed. She understood that the outcome of the situation was entirely in the Lord's hands, and she called upon her fellow Jews to join her in prayer and fasting for the Lord's deliverance.

IF I PERISH, I PERISH: Here we see the true nature of Esther's heart: she was fully committed to obeying God, even if it meant sacrificing her life in the process.

⤳ READING ESTHER 5:1–4 ⤳

FINDING FAVOR WITH THE KING: *After three days of prayer and fasting, Esther puts her life on the line and enters the king's presence unbidden. His response will have profound consequences.*

1. THE KING SAT ON HIS ROYAL THRONE: God was in control even over such small details as where the king sat and which direction he was facing the moment Esther entered the courtyard. In this situation, Esther was able to stand afar off from the king and wait for him to see her.

2. SHE FOUND FAVOR IN HIS SIGHT: Esther found favor in the sight of the king because she had first found favor in the sight of God (Proverbs 21:1).

3. IT SHALL BE GIVEN TO YOU: From a human perspective, the tables suddenly turned for Esther and the Jews at this moment, as the queen found favor with the king. But the truth is that the tables were never against God's people in the first place, for God had His sovereign hand upon all events from before the beginning of time.

4. THE BANQUET THAT I HAVE PREPARED: We will see what transpired after this in the next study.

⌁ FIRST IMPRESSIONS ⌁

1. *If you had been in Esther's place, how would you have reacted when the king commanded you to become his concubine? How would you have reacted in Mordecai's place?*

2. *How did Esther react to becoming part of the king's harem? How did she not react? What does this reveal about her character?*

3. *What people came to look on Esther with favor in these passages? Why? What part did Esther play in that process? What part did God play?*

4. *Why did Esther not request anything from the king's treasures when she had the opportunity (2:15)? What did this reveal about her character?*

⌁ Some Key Principles ⌁

God puts us where He wants us for His specific purposes.

A young Jewish woman named Esther found herself suddenly whisked from complete obscurity to become queen of the world's most powerful empire. Daniel went from being a prisoner of war to being the most trusted counselor of another powerful world ruler. Joseph rocketed from a prison pit to the throne of Egypt, yet another of the world's most powerful nations. It is easy, in retrospect, to see God's sovereign hand in such instances because they are so dramatic and miraculous.

Yet the same principle is always at work in the mundane, day-to-day realities of our lives. Esther was indeed whisked to the throne, but before that could happen she had to endure being wrenched from her home and family and married without having her own inclinations considered. Year after year, Mordecai worked a steady job that probably did not seem very dramatic or miraculous from day to day—yet the Lord had placed him exactly where he needed to be. Even Daniel had to endure a lengthy period of uncertainty and danger before he saw God's miraculous blessings.

The fact is that, before God could reveal His miraculous plans for these people, they were called upon to be faithful to some less-dramatic occupation for a period of time. The same principle holds true in our lives today: God has placed each of His children exactly where He wants them to be in order to work out a bigger plan in their lives and in the lives of others. Esther and Mordecai and others could not see the future of what God intended to do through them, and neither can we. Our job is to work diligently and faithfully wherever the Lord has placed us; He'll take care of the future.

You might not learn the reason why.

It is tempting to focus on the honors and gifts Esther received when she entered the king's household, overlooking the hardship that must have been involved. She had been taken away from a godly home with no regard to her desires and was forced to live among women who had no knowledge of God or His commands. She spent at least a year in the women's quarters at the king's palace in an atmosphere that must have been highly charged with jealousy, envy, and competition. She had no idea who would be chosen as queen, and probably spent many sleepless nights wishing she could be back home with her cousin Mordecai.

Then one day, the Lord's plan was revealed to her—or at least part of it—when she was crowned as the king's new wife. Five years passed, during which she might well have assumed that she had come to a full understanding of the Lord's reason for taking her away from Mordecai's household. But the fullness of His plan had not yet been revealed, as she discovered after Haman hatched his diabolical plot. As Mordecai pointed out, "Who knows whether you have come to the kingdom for such a time as this?" (Esther 4:14). She did not come to understand the Lord's purposes until years had passed from the time of her hardship.

It is very encouraging when one can look back upon times of hardship and see how the Lord used the difficulties for His glory and our blessing; but we must also understand that the Lord does not always explain His reasons to us. Times of uncertainty and hardship require faith, a solid conviction that God is in control and is working out His perfect plan in our lives—even when we cannot understand what that plan is. The writer of Hebrews defines faith as "the substance of things hoped for, the evidence of things not seen" (Hebrews 11:1). The "hope" in this verse refers not to a wish that something might happen in the future but to a firm belief that God will keep His promises, working all things together for our good and His glory (Romans 8:28). We may not see what God's purpose is at present; indeed, we might not see His greatest purpose until eternity. But we can rest in the faith that His plan is being worked out, and the suffering will be nothing compared with the glory to be revealed. Our confidence is founded on His character.

When facing a trial, remind yourself that God is in control.

This principle flows naturally from the previous one. Esther must have been caught off guard, to say the least, when she was informed of her impending marriage to the king of Persia—regardless of her own desires. Certainly, Daniel felt fear and sorrow as he was carried forcibly away from his home as a prisoner of war. Even Mordecai must have been grieved and fearful as his beloved cousin was led off to join the king's concubines, sequestered in quarters where no man was permitted.

Yet Mordecai's words to Esther summarize the attitude that God's people should adopt whenever difficulties arise: "Relief and deliverance will arise. . . . Yet who knows whether you have come to the kingdom for such a time as this?" (Esther 4:14). Who can say what purpose the Lord is working toward through your present time of trial? Like Esther and Mordecai and many others who have endured trials, we must cling firmly to the knowledge that God is in control and is faithfully working out a plan for our blessing.

All we can be certain of at such times is this one unalterable fact: relief and deliverance will arise, and God will always prove faithful to His people. It can be easy to forget this important truth when trials are raging about us, yet those are the very times when remembering this principle is the most vital. The author of Hebrews reminds us to draw near to God "with a true heart in full assurance of faith, having our hearts sprinkled from an evil conscience and our bodies washed with pure water. Let us hold fast the confession of our hope without wavering, for He who promised is faithful" (Hebrews 10:22–23).

Find favor in God's eyes, and don't worry about the favor of men.

The men and women in these studies have all demonstrated an overriding characteristic in their lives: they were all concerned primarily with finding favor in God's eyes. Daniel and his friends refrained from eating food sacrificed to idols simply because it was forbidden by God's Word. Esther and Mordecai had developed a lifetime habit of obeying God that enabled them to keep a godly perspective in the face of unexpected trials.

Yet in each case, these men and women were also faced with the risk of losing favor in the eyes of men—and sometimes in danger of the king's fearsome wrath as well. Daniel's refusal to eat the forbidden foods set him at odds with the king's direct commands. Esther faced an instant death sentence by entering the king's presence uninvited, while Mordecai also faced death for actions we'll look at in future studies. But they were all willing to risk the king's wrath because they had set a higher priority on obeying God's Word than on pleasing men.

It is no coincidence that these men and women also found favor with the king in the long run, even though they had gone against the pressures of the world around them—for "when a man's ways please the LORD, He makes even his enemies to be at peace with him" (Proverbs 16:7). As Christians, our priority is always to be doing the will of the Father and striving to please Him in all our ways. James warns us, "Do you not know that friendship with the world is enmity with God? Whoever therefore wants to be a friend of the world makes himself an enemy of God" (James 4:4).

⁂ DIGGING DEEPER ⁂

5. *Why did Esther not reveal the fact that she was a Jew? When should a Christian make his faith known openly to others?*

6. *Why did Esther fast? Why did she ask others to join her in that fast? What part does fasting play in prayer and intercession?*

7. *What ways can you see God's sovereign hand in the events of this study?*

8. *What purposes might God have for placing you where you are at present? What task might He have for you to fulfill? What are you doing to accomplish that?*

↜ Taking It Personally ↝

9. *Are you presently facing a situation where it's hard to see God's sovereign hand? How can you deliberately remind yourself this week that He is in control?*

10. *Which is generally the focus of your thinking: the opinions of others, or the opinion of God? What areas of your life might need to be reassessed in light of God's opinion?*

~ 5 ~
PRESERVING GOD'S PEOPLE

↶ HISTORICAL BACKGROUND ↷

During the time of Israel's exodus from Egypt, nearly a thousand years before our study opens, the Amalekites (descendants of Esau) sent out their army to attack the people of Israel without provocation. The Lord declared at that time that He would wipe out the Amalekites from existence for their betrayal of God's people. Hundreds of years later, the Lord had commanded King Saul to carry out that sentence by exterminating the entire nation of Amalek—but he did not obey fully. He did kill most of the people, but he kept the best of their possessions for himself, and he allowed the Amalekite king, Agag, to remain alive. (See book 6 in this series, *Prophets, Priests, and Kings*, for more information on this event.)

In this study, we will meet a descendant of King Agag named Haman, who had been promoted to a very high position of authority in the government of the Persian Empire. The king had made Haman second to himself, much as Pharaoh had done for Joseph nearly fifteen hundred years earlier. There was, however, a very striking difference between Haman and Joseph: Haman hated the Jews. We will discover that Saul's disobedience continued to have ramifications for God's people more than five hundred years later.

The laws of Persia made it impossible for a decree from the king to be repealed; once a law was written, it remained in effect permanently. Imagine, then, how devastating it would be if a law were written making it legal—indeed, a requirement—to murder all the Jews living in the kingdom. That is precisely what happened during Queen Esther's reign. As we will see in this study, the Lord is sovereign over all the affairs of mankind, and He is not bound by any nation's laws. These events also led to the annual celebration of Purim, which Jewish people still observe today.

ᴧ Reading Esther 3:8–15 ᴧ

Haman's Plot: *A man named Haman is promoted to high office by the king, and he uses that position to carry out his hatred against the people of God.*

8. Haman said to King Ahasuerus: The king had recently promoted Haman to a position of high favor, ordering that all people should bow before Haman wherever he went. Mordecai, however, refused to do so, increasing the animosity that comes to a head in this study. These events took place in 474 BC, approximately five years after Esther entered the king's household.

they do not keep the king's laws: The first part of Haman's claim may have been true, that the Jews observed laws that seemed strange to the Persians as they undertook to obey God's commands, but this second statement was a pure lie. By mixing fact with falsehood, Haman made his scheme seem more legitimate to the king. His tactic was to couch his wicked plan in terms of protecting the king from potential rebellion, pretending to be looking out for national interests rather than personal vendetta.

9. they be destroyed: Haman was not merely trying to get revenge on Mordecai; he had an overriding hatred of the entire Jewish race. We will discover that his ancestors had nursed a hatred of the Jews dating back to the time of King Saul. Haman was carrying out a deliberate plan of genocide based on an ancient malice toward the people of God.

ten thousand talents of silver: This was a huge sum, amounting to approximately 375 tons of silver! Greek historian Herodotus wrote that the annual royal income of the Persian Empire was fifteen thousand talents, so this was equal to two-thirds of the national tax revenues. Haman did not intend to pay it out of his own funds, but to loot it from the murdered Jews—which suggests also that the Jews had grown fairly prosperous during their exile in Persia.

10. signet ring: The king's ring had a unique seal engraved upon it, which he would impress into hot wax on official decrees. Giving that ring to another person demonstrated absolute trust, and the king gave Haman authority equal to his own.

Ancient Animosity: *Haman is a descendant of King Agag, last king of the Amalekites, who were destroyed by Israel. He is still motivated by that ancient grudge.*

THE AGAGITE: Here we gain a very important bit of information about Haman: he was descended from Agag, who had been the king of the Amalekites more than five hundred years earlier, during the time of King Saul. The Lord had commanded Saul to utterly destroy the Amalekites, but he had only partially obeyed, killing the people but keeping the best of their possessions for himself—and allowing King Agag to live. Samuel had stepped in and killed Agag, but evidently members of his immediate family escaped. (See 1 Samuel 15 for the entire account.) Haman's hatred of the Jews amounted to a national prejudice that had been nursed for hundreds of years.

THE ENEMY OF THE JEWS: The Amalekites were descendants from Esau. When Israel was making their way toward the promised land after leaving Egypt, the Amalekites attacked them unprovoked. The Lord gave Israel victory that day and promised to "utterly blot out the remembrance of Amalek from under heaven" (Exodus 17:14). Haman was continuing the animosity between the people of Israel and his own forebears; ironically, his hatred was actually bringing about the fulfillment of God's promise.

12. THE THIRTEENTH DAY OF THE FIRST MONTH: This date has been calculated to be April 7, 474 BC.

13. TO DESTROY, TO KILL, AND TO ANNIHILATE ALL THE JEWS: This decree mirrors the Lord's command to Saul concerning the Amalekites (1 Samuel 15:3). It was no coincidence that Haman was trying to do to the Jews what the Lord had commanded Israel to do to his ancestors.

THE THIRTEENTH DAY OF THE TWELFTH MONTH: That is, March 7, 473 BC. Haman was allowing a full year for the people to prepare for their one day of slaughter. Also, the Persian Empire was so large that it would take time for the king's decree to reach its borders.

15. THE CITY OF SHUSHAN WAS PERPLEXED: "Perplexed" is actually an amusing understatement. Imagine the confusion and chaos that would ensue if a king today suddenly commanded all his subjects to wantonly murder every Jew on a certain day next year and loot their homes—and to do so not only without fear of punishment, but out of obedience to the law!

⌁ READING ESTHER 7:1–10 ⌁

ESTHER'S REQUEST: *Queen Esther holds two banquets for the king and Haman, and at the second one she makes her request to save the Jews from annihilation.*

1. WENT TO DINE WITH QUEEN ESTHER: This is not the banquet mentioned at the end of the last study (5:4), but a second one on the following day.

3. LET MY LIFE BE GIVEN ME: The king did not know at this point that Esther was a Jew, but Haman had also carefully failed to mention who the people were that he intended to exterminate. The king had been unwise in giving Haman such carte blanche in his decree, but now the truth was coming to light.

4. WE HAVE BEEN SOLD: This suggests that the king's motivation in permitting Haman's outrageous decree may have been mercenary, lured into the indiscretion by Haman's huge offer of silver. Esther finally revealed that she was a Jew, but more importantly she openly identified herself with the people of God. If the king chose to go forward with the extermination of the Jews, Esther was determined to share their fate.

THE ENEMY COULD NEVER COMPENSATE FOR THE KING'S LOSS: This suggests that Esther was appealing to the king's mercenary self-interest as Haman had done, pointing out that the Jews would be worth more alive in the long run than Haman's huge bribe. Other Bibles translate this phrase somewhat differently, however, suggesting that it would not have been worthwhile to bother the king with such a small matter as the enslavement of the Jews. Either way, Esther was making it clear to the king that he was going to suffer loss from Haman's wicked scheme.

HAMAN'S DOWNFALL: *In one sudden moment, the Lord turns Haman's wicked schemes away from the Jews and toward his own household.*

7. THE KING AROSE IN HIS WRATH: King Ahasuerus was suddenly confronted with the realization that he had once again been persuaded by his courtiers to endanger his own queen. He had already sacrificed his marriage to Vashti at their advice; now he stood to lose his beloved Esther as well. His wrath was undoubtedly doubled by the fact that Haman had persuaded him through deceit, betraying the great trust he had freely bestowed.

THE PALACE GARDEN: Once again we see the Lord's sovereign hand guiding the smallest details in this remarkable series of events. The king stormed out of the room in order to regain his composure and think clearly about what to do in the situation (Haman's decree was irreversible, which put the king in a difficult spot), but his absence gave Haman the chance to throw himself at the queen's feet—literally, as it turned out.

8. HAMAN HAD FALLEN ACROSS THE COUCH: Haman's sudden reversal of position, from king's favorite to king's enemy, disconcerted him, and he evidently lost his balance while pleading for his life. His position on the queen's couch was enough to forfeit his life, for Persian law dictated that no man except chosen eunuchs could ever be alone with any woman of the king's household—yet here was Haman, not only alone but lying with her on her couch! In that moment, his fate was sealed.

THEY COVERED HAMAN'S FACE: Condemned prisoners were not permitted to look upon the king. Those condemned to death in the ancient world would have their heads covered upon hearing the sentence so that their last view of this world would be of the judge pronouncing their doom.

9. THE GALLOWS . . . WHICH HAMAN MADE FOR MORDECAI: The Lord had caused the king to learn, just that day, that Mordecai had saved him from a rebellious plot; even as he was discovering Mordecai's loyalty, Haman was building a gallows. The Lord had every event perfectly under control, even when things appeared hopeless.

10. THEY HANGED HAMAN ON THE GALLOWS THAT HE HAD PREPARED FOR MORDECAI: Haman's treacherous plans backfired against himself. This is the final result for anyone who attempts to defy God; and just as surely, all who obey God will enjoy His protection and sovereign guidance. (We will learn how Haman's decree was reversed in Study 9.)

ᕼ FIRST IMPRESSIONS ᕼ

1. In what ways did Haman deceive the king regarding the Jews? How did this happen? How might the king have ruled more wisely in that situation?

2. What motivated Haman to try to annihilate the Jews? Where did his deep hatred come from? Was he justified for feeling that way?

3. *If you had been a Jew in Persia at this time, how would you have reacted to Haman's decree? How would you have reacted if you'd been a Gentile at the time?*

4. *In what ways can you see God's sovereign hand guiding the events of these passages? What does this teach about His sovereignty in the affairs of your own life?*

↜ Some Key Principles ↝

Treat others the way you'd like to be treated.

Haman provides a stark contrast to the lives of Esther and Mordecai. He was a man who looked out for his own interests at all times, striving to glorify himself and to destroy his enemies. He urged the king to bestow unprecedented honors when he thought it was for himself (ironically bestowing them instead on Mordecai), while simultaneously building a giant gallows on which to hang his enemy. He embodied the world's primary teaching: "Look out for number one."

God's Word, however, teaches a very different principle: treat others better than you treat yourself. Solomon warned against Haman's way of life when he wrote, "Whoever digs a pit will fall into it, and he who rolls a stone will have it roll back on him" (Proverbs 26:27). Haman's own gallows were used to hang not only himself but his sons. Paul commanded his readers to adopt the opposite attitude: "Let nothing be done through selfish ambition or conceit, but in lowliness of mind let each esteem others better than himself" (Philippians 2:3).

The Lord Jesus summed up this principle in what we commonly call the Golden Rule: "But I say to you who hear: Love your enemies, do good to those who hate you, bless those who curse you, and pray for those who spitefully use you. To him who strikes you on the one cheek, offer the other also. And from him who takes away your cloak, do not withhold your tunic either. Give to everyone who asks of you. And from him who takes away your goods do not ask them back. And just as you want men to do to you, you also do to them likewise" (Luke 6:27–31).

The Lord protects His people.

The Jews were threatened by an overwhelming foe. Haman had been elevated to a position that effectively made him one of the most powerful men in the world. When the king handed him his signet ring, he had the ability to write laws that could not be reversed; whatever he chose to do would be put into effect throughout the Persian Empire, and there was nobody who could speak against him. From a human perspective, the people of God were powerless against this man who hated them, and his decree to annihilate them spelled the end for the nation of Israel.

But God is infinitely more powerful than any human being or nation on earth, and there is no one who can stand against His sovereign control. The great news is that God has promised to care for those who obey His Word, for those who have accepted His gift of salvation through His Son, Jesus Christ. Each Christian is sealed by the Holy Spirit; each bears the image of Jesus, which can never be removed. We belong to God, and He will protect us from those who seek our harm.

Paul addressed our sealing when he wrote to the Corinthians, "Now He who establishes us with you in Christ and has anointed us is God, who also has sealed us and given us the Spirit in our hearts as a guarantee" (2 Corinthians 1:21–22). This is the guarantee of our eternal inheritance, one that will never fail. As we've seen throughout our studies, the Lord might call us at times to endure persecution, but in the end He will never permit the enemy to do us eternal harm. "Because you have kept My command to persevere," the Lord said to the church at Philadelphia, "I also will keep you from the hour of trial which shall come upon the whole world, to test those who dwell on the earth. Behold, I am coming quickly! Hold fast what you have, that no one may take your crown" (Revelation 3:10–11). Our job is to obey His Word, and He will take care of the rest.

Christians should not be surprised by persecution.

This principle is the other side to the previous one. In times of trial the Lord will protect His children from the evil one, but that does not necessarily mean we will never suffer persecution. Esther and Mordecai—indeed, all the Jews living in Persia—were called by God to endure a time of danger and terrific threat. Though that threat was never realized, God's people in other ages have endured more, being called even to face martyrdom at the hands of their enemies.

We must remember that the things of this world will all come to an end—including our earthly lives, possessions, and welfare. There have been times throughout history when the Lord called upon His people to sacrifice those things for His sake, even to the point of shedding their own blood and losing their lives. There are Christians even today who face imprisonment and loss for the sake of the gospel, and believers in the West should not be caught by surprise if the same should happen to them. Yet as we have seen repeatedly in these studies, the Lord is faithful to strengthen and guide His servants through such times, just as He guided Daniel, Mordecai, Esther, and others.

The reason for such persecution is that the world hates Christ; and if it hates Christ, it will also hate those who belong to Him. Jesus warned His disciples, "If the world hates you, you know that it hated Me before it hated you. If you were of the world, the world would love its own. Yet because you are not of the world, but I chose you out of the world, therefore the world hates you. Remember the word that I said to you, 'A servant is not greater than his master.' If they persecuted Me, they will also persecute you" (John 15:18–20). Do not be surprised if you suffer for being a Christian, but consider it an honor, for then you are sharing in the sufferings of Christ.

ᴧ DIGGING DEEPER ᴧ

5. Read 1 Samuel 15:1–3, 9. What were the long-range consequences of Saul's failure to obey God's command to completely destroy the Amalekites? What does this teach about the importance of complete obedience?

6. How might this story have been different if Haman had treated others the way he liked being treated himself? How does this illustrate Jesus' commands?

7. Why did the Lord allow His people to suffer from Haman's persecution? How did He protect them? What does this teach about the suffering of Christians?

8. When have you suffered persecution for your faith in Christ? How did you respond to it? How might you respond differently in the future?

9. When have you recently treated someone in a way that you would not like being treated yourself? How can you make amends?

10. Take time each day this week to pray for Christians in foreign lands, such as China, who are suffering for their faith in Christ.

Section 2:

Characters

IN THIS SECTION:

～ 6 ～
DANIEL'S FRIENDS

DANIEL 3

⋏ CHARACTERS' BACKGROUND ⋏

We now move back in time to around 580 BC when King Nebuchadnezzar was ruling in Babylon. In Study 1, we met Daniel's three friends Hananiah, Mishael, and Azariah, whose names had been changed to Shadrach, Meshach, and Abed-Nego. Approximately twenty years had passed since Daniel interpreted the king's dream, and these three young men had grown into adults. As he did with Daniel, the king had entrusted them with positions of responsibility in Babylon, and it would appear that they were well-known and respected.

The Lord had blessed His faithful servants with success and responsibility, and things appeared to be going well. They were important members of the court, serving the most powerful monarch on earth in a city that was world renowned for its beauty and man-made wonders. Who would want to rock the boat in such a situation? Leave well enough alone, as the world's motto goes; just go with the flow, and don't draw attention to yourself.

But what does a godly person do when the civil authorities command him to disobey the Word of God? Believers are commanded to submit to human authority; what happens when that authority defies God? This is precisely the situation that arose for these three men when the king constructed a giant statue and commanded them to bow down and worship it. Shadrach, Meshach, and Abed-Nego were forced to choose whom to obey, God or man, and that choice brought dire consequences. But as we'll see in this study, God remains ever-faithful to those who obey His Word.

⋏ READING DANIEL 3:1–30 ⋏

THE GOLDEN IMAGE: *Nebuchadnezzar builds a statue that is somewhat reminiscent of the one he dreamed about in Study 2—except that this time he commands people to worship it.*

1. Nebuchadnezzar the king: We now return to the time of Daniel, roughly one hundred years prior to the time of Esther, around 580 BC.

Sixty cubits . . . six cubits: A cubit was eighteen to twenty inches in length, depending upon whether the measurements were Israelite or Babylonian. The statue was between ninety and one hundred feet tall by nine or ten feet wide. The image of the man probably stood atop a large pedestal, which would have made the statue itself of normal human proportions. We are not told whose image it was; perhaps Nebuchadnezzar himself, or perhaps an image of Nabu, a false deity worshiped in Babylon (the first part of Nebuchadnezzar's name).

He set it up in the plain of Dura: There are several overtones implicit in Nebuchadnezzar's statue. First, it is reminiscent of the dream he had earlier that depicted the form of a man made of gold, silver, bronze, iron, and clay. That image, however, represented Babylon and the kingdoms to follow, while Nebuchadnezzar's statue seems to imply that there would be no other kingdoms to follow Nebuchadnezzar's "golden reign." Second, the giant statue standing alone in a plain is reminiscent of the Tower of Babel (Genesis 11), another man-made object intended to declare the glory of man's accomplishments.

3. the image that King Nebuchadnezzar had set up: Notice how frequently this phrase is used in the chapter, emphasizing the fact that a man-made object was being raised up for people to worship.

5. you shall fall down and worship the gold image: Here is the point where the king's law transgressed the laws of God. We have seen in other studies that God's people are to obey their earthly authorities, but there can come a time when those authorities command God's people to disobey His Word, and at that point their authority ceases to be binding.

6. whoever does not fall down and worship: It is important to remember that, in the views of the ancient Middle East, such a law would not have been considered tyrannical. The pagan nations believed that one could freely offer homage to one deity while still remaining faithful to another; so a worshiper of Baal, for example, might not feel any compunction about also bowing in worship before this idol. But God commands His people to worship Him alone and to refrain from bowing before any false idols. This is why the Jews would have stood out as unique and rebellious in their refusal to bow before Nebuchadnezzar's image.

Refusing to Bow Down: *Daniel's three friends, whom we met in Study 1, have refused to bow before the statue. Their faith is about to be put to the test.*

8. **Chaldeans:** The magicians and so-called wise men whom we met in Study 2.

accused the Jews: The Hebrew translated "accused" is actually a phrase that could be transliterated as "devoured piecemeal." The image is of a ravening beast ripping apart its prey in a feeding frenzy. Once again, the Jews were faced with enemies who hated them and sought to chew them up.

12. **Shadrach, Meshach, and Abed-Nego:** These are Hananiah, Mishael, and Azariah, whom we met in Study 1. They went through the same training process as Daniel, in which they refused to eat the forbidden foods, and now we find that, like Daniel, they had risen to prominent roles within the kingdom of Babylon.

have not paid due regard to you: These three men were faced with a difficult situation. The king's law commanded them to disobey God's law, so they were forced to choose whom to obey. By obeying God's commands, they had to disobey the king's commands—which was seen as an open rebellion against his authority.

13. **in rage and fury:** It is interesting to see the way in which God's enemies were able to stir up the rage of kings against God's people. We saw this in the previous study, where Haman deceived the king into commanding the death of his own queen, and here we see another king being coerced into throwing loyal servants into the furnace.

14. **Is it true:** Nebuchadnezzar at least demonstrated more wisdom than Ahasuerus at this point by investigating the truth of the accusations.

15. **who is the god who will deliver you from my hands:** Nevertheless, Nebuchadnezzar was still deceived by his own pride, thinking that he was more powerful than Almighty God. He was about to learn the answer to his own question.

16. **we have no need to answer you in this matter:** That is to say, "We have no defense to offer against these accusations." The three men were not being disrespectful; they were acknowledging that the accusations were true in that they had refused to bow before the image. They were also letting the king know that their actions had been carefully considered, and they had no need to reconsider now—they were firmly committed to not worship the idol.

17. **our God whom we serve is able to deliver us:** The men answered the king's rhetorical question, telling him clearly that their God was indeed able to save them out of his hand.

18. **But if not:** The men also recognized that the Lord might allow them to die in that fiery furnace. As we have seen already, the Lord sometimes allows His servants to experience suffering and even death for His name. Yet the men trusted Him so completely that they were willing to follow His sovereign guidance, even to the point of a gruesome death by fire.

BURNING WITH RAGE: *Nebuchadnezzar's wrath flares up as hot as his furnace at the men's defiance, and he has them bound and thrown into the flames.*

19. NEBUCHADNEZZAR WAS FULL OF FURY: The author emphasized the great wrath of the king, underscoring the fact that his rage was leading him into sin rather than wise leadership. His wrath was stirred not by discovering unrighteousness but by having his will frustrated by the very righteousness of the three men that led them to resist his ungodly demands.

THE EXPRESSION ON HIS FACE CHANGED: The Hebrew word translated *expression* is the same used for the *image* that Nebuchadnezzar created. The king's pride and willfulness had become an idol in his own life, like a stubborn child accustomed to getting his own way.

HEAT THE FURNACE SEVEN TIMES MORE: That is, make the furnace as hot as it possibly can be. Ironically, this would have been merciful, as it would have led to a quicker death—if that were what the Lord had willed.

21. THE BURNING FIERY FURNACE: Bricks were the generic building material used in Babylon, and brick kilns were often quite large, tall enough for men to walk inside. Little else is known of the furnaces, however. Some of the details suggest it was a vertical, pipelike structure; for example, the guards "took up" the three men to cast them in. Other details suggest a horizontal structure; for example, the king was seated nearby, looking inside (where a vertical structure would have been too hot to look down on). Regardless, bricks are baked at sixteen hundred to two thousand degrees Fahrenheit.

22. THE FLAME OF THE FIRE KILLED THOSE MEN: King Nebuchadnezzar had boasted that no god could save Daniel's friends from his hand, but the truth was that the king could not save his own men from the hand of God.

THE FLAMES HAVE NO POWER: *Suddenly the king realizes that something is amiss—there are four men in the furnace instead of three!*

25. THE FOURTH IS LIKE THE SON OF GOD: We are not told whether this was an angel or God Himself. It is quite possible that this is a theophany, an appearance of God in human form prior to the birth of Christ. Nebuchadnezzar, of course, was not aware of the triune nature of God—Father, Son, and Holy Spirit—yet even this idolatrous king could not deny the presence and involvement of Almighty God in the lives of these three men.

26. servants of the Most High God: The testimony of these three men, their faith in God and open testimony to His power, led a pagan king to publicly acknowledge the Most High God. His words confessed that Israel's God was supreme, able to save those whom He chose out of the hands of their enemies. He was retracting his earlier boast that no god could save the men from his powerful hand.

Shadrach, Meshach, and Abed-Nego came from the midst of the fire: The three men had been unable to walk under their own power when they were thrown into the fire, but God's hand of salvation had set them completely free so that they could walk out unbound.

27. the fire had no power: The powers of this world are powerless against the sovereignty of God, and the dangers that God's people face cannot touch them without His permission.

the smell of fire was not on them: Here is another small picture of the salvation afforded through Christ. Fire is frequently used in Scripture to represent the wrath of God, but Christians are redeemed out of His terrible wrath to the extent that there is not even a whiff of judgment on our souls.

28. Blessed be the God of Shadrach, Meshach, and Abed-Nego: It is significant that Nebuchadnezzar gave glory to God rather than to some power the men might have possessed. Their open testimony to God's power and faithfulness left no room for him to think that they had saved themselves, and he was forced to confess that God was present in their lives.

yielded their bodies: Daniel's three friends had yielded their entire beings to God's sovereign hand, even to the point of submitting to death in order to obey His Word.

29. the God of Shadrach, Meshach, and Abed-Nego: Nebuchadnezzar had gained knowledge of the true God through the testimony of Daniel's friends, but he had not yet reached the point of making Him his own God. We will witness this final conversion in the next study.

ᴗ First Impressions ᴗ

1. *What might have motivated Nebuchadnezzar to create the giant statue? Why would he command people to worship it?*

2. *What would you have done if you'd been commanded to worship the king's statue? What would you have done when confronted, as Daniel's friends were?*

3. *Why did Nebuchadnezzar's anger flare up in this passage? What lay behind his anger? How did it affect his judgment?*

4. *When is it right to disobey earthly authorities? When is it wrong? How can a Christian discern the difference?*

⤳ Some Key Principles ⤳

Man's wrath does not produce God's righteousness.

It would appear that King Nebuchadnezzar's temper was modeled after his furnaces: fiery! His magicians asked to know what his dream was before offering an interpretation, and he roared, "If you do not make known the dream to me, and its interpretation, you shall be cut in pieces, and your houses shall be made an ash heap" (Daniel 2:5). His rage flared up instantly when his will was thwarted, and his punishments were extreme. Even after he realized that Daniel's friends served Almighty God, he resorted to his old threat of cutting in pieces any who spoke ill of God, making their houses as ash heaps.

The truth is that Nebuchadnezzar's anger was a natural consequence of his pride, not a righteous indignation against defiance or unlawful behavior. It was his pride that led him to create the golden image and command his nation to worship it, and that pride was offended when Daniel's friends refused to comply. His subsequent anger clouded his judgment, and he ended up defying the God of creation. If the king had humbled himself and cooled his anger, he might have recognized that the men's testimony was true and that his image was nothing more than a false god.

James warned his readers of the deadly trap of human wrath: "So then, my beloved brethren, let every man be swift to hear, slow to speak, slow to wrath; for the wrath of man does not produce the righteousness of God" (James 1:19–20). The Lord had raised up Daniel's friends as a witness to the king, offering him the chance to hear the truth concerning his idolatrous practices—but he refused to listen. Instead, he was quick to speak and quick to indulge his wrath, and as a result he quickly fell into deadly error. When anger flares up, take time to listen and pray. Quick speech can result in negative long-term consequences.

God's Word takes precedence over human laws.

We have seen in previous studies how God's people had a high respect for those in authority over them. Esther maintained a humble and submissive spirit, which led her authorities to find favor with her. Daniel and his friends humbly suggested an alternative diet plan rather than defiantly going on a hunger strike, and the Lord blessed that plan with great success. Indeed, all these people rose to positions of prominence in the courts of various kings, and that alone indicates that they were always submissive and respectful to authorities; it is rare, after all, that a person is promoted if he has an attitude of rebellion.

But there also can come a time when human authorities command God's people to violate His Word, and at that point a believer must choose who has the higher authority: God or man. Daniel's friends found themselves in just that position when the king commanded them to worship an idol. Nebuchadnezzar had done nothing wrong when he created the statue; it was his command to worship it that violated God's Word, and at that point Daniel's friends stood up—quite literally.

Paul reminds us that Christians are commanded to obey human authorities, because they have been placed in authority by God Himself (Romans 13:1–7). Yet Peter and others were commanded by the high priest to not preach the gospel in Jerusalem, forcing them to choose between the commands of God and men. "But Peter and the other apostles answered and said: 'We ought to obey God rather than men'" (Acts 5:29). The reason Peter refused to obey the high priest was the same reason Daniel's friends refused to bow: the human authorities had commanded them to violate a clearly defined commandment of God. The principle is this: obey human authorities in all things, except when such obedience would force you to violate a clear principle of Scripture. It is at that point, and that point only, where human authority ceases to be binding.

No danger can touch us without God's permission.

From the world's perspective, Daniel's three friends must have appeared foolishly overconfident, even self-deluded, and out of touch with reality in their answer to King Nebuchadnezzar. That furnace looming before them was terribly real, as were the flames that leaped and danced out of its mouth. Those flames were so hot that they consumed those who dared to get too close, never mind being thrown inside, yet Shadrach, Meshach, and Abed-Nego remained calmly steadfast in their determination to not bow before the king's idol.

Those three men knew full well that the flames were real, but they also understood that those flames were under the sovereign command of their Creator. If God so chose, not a hair on their heads would be singed—which proved to be exactly the case. Yet the men also understood that the sovereign Lord of creation could equally choose to let the flames take their natural course, consuming their bodies even as they consumed the guards. They remained steadfast just the same because they trusted that the Lord's decision in the matter would be the best conclusion, whether they continued to live in this world or passed through death into the eternal presence of their Lord and King.

Their attitude is a model for all believers to follow, remembering that God is absolutely faithful to His children; He will not permit anything to touch us that is not ultimately for our good. As the psalmist wrote, "My help comes from the LORD, who made heaven and earth. He will not allow your foot to be moved; He who keeps you will not slumber. Behold, He who keeps Israel shall neither slumber nor sleep. The LORD is your keeper; the LORD is your shade at your right hand. The sun shall not strike you by day, nor the moon by night. The LORD shall preserve you from all evil; He shall preserve your soul. The LORD shall preserve your going out and your coming in from this time forth, and even forevermore" (Psalm 121:2–8).

Christians bear witness by both word and deed.

There is no record that when King Nebuchadnezzar built his giant statue, any of his subjects spoke out against the project. As far as we know, there were no organized protests; no people marching in the streets, carrying signs; no newspaper editorials denouncing the project. Neither is there any record of protest against the king's wicked edict, demanding that his subjects bow and worship before that statue. Quite the contrary, in fact: "all the people, nations, and languages fell down and worshiped the gold image which King Nebuchadnezzar had set up" (v. 7), evidently without comment.

Of course, public dissent and organized protests are a thing of modern times, not the stuff of an absolute monarchy under a king like Nebuchadnezzar. Yet the point here is that Daniel's friends did not march before the king to speak out against his decree—yet they still bore a powerful witness for the truth of God's Word. They bore that witness visually rather than audibly, through their deeds more than through their words. When the king challenged them on their behavior, they did not hesitate to speak words of truth, but it was their steadfast refusal to bow—their overt actions in the sight of the world around them—that bore the most convincing testimony to God's righteousness.

The principle here is that actions are as important as words. Daniel's friends might have gone about expounding on God's commands against worshiping idols, but if they had then bowed down at the king's command, those words would have lost their power. It was the deeds of Daniel's friends that demonstrated the saving power of God, and their willingness to be thrown into a fiery furnace out of obedience more than the words they spoke beforehand. James sums this up: "Faith by itself, if it does not have works, is dead" (James 2:17). Daniel's friends verbally expressed their faith in God's power to save, but they also had to *act* on those words before God's power was shown to the world. Christians should be quick to speak the words of God, but if they don't also live by those words, then their words become a dead faith.

⤳ DIGGING DEEPER ⤳

5. *Put the answer of Daniel's friends (v. 16–18) into your own words. Why did they refuse to bow down? Why were they so calm in that situation?*

6. How did their testimony influence King Nebuchadnezzar? How did it influence the world around them?

7. Why might God have chosen to keep these men alive in the furnace? When in the Bible did He allow His servants to succumb to death? What purposes did He have in each case?

8. Why did a fourth man appear in the furnace with Daniel's friends? What does this teach about God's involvement in your own trials?

⌁ Taking It Personally ⌁

9. What hardships or trials are you dealing with at present? How can the experience of Daniel's friends help you in facing that situation?

10. How do you generally deal with anger? When has your anger hindered God's righteousness? What can you learn from Nebuchadnezzar's example?

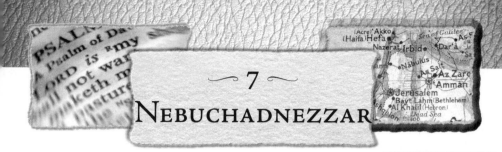

7

NEBUCHADNEZZAR

DANIEL 4

∽ CHARACTER'S BACKGROUND ∽

Babylon was the most powerful and wealthy nation of its day, and the empire extended throughout the Middle East. King Nebuchadnezzar and his father had increased its borders and prestige dramatically, until every nation and language of the day came under its influence. Nebuchadnezzar, like Solomon, also undertook many ambitious building projects in his capital city, fortifying Babylon with an extensive system of walls and creating beautiful temples, roads and bridges, palaces, gates, and even a ziggurat (a towerlike temple similar to the Tower of Babel). He created a remarkable hanging garden that became one of the seven wonders of the ancient world.

In the process, he also became proud. He stood atop his huge palace walls and gazed out upon his realm, quite literally master of all he surveyed, and he told himself that he had accomplished it all through his own majesty and might. He saw himself as an omnipotent sovereign—but God saw him quite differently. In this study, we will discover that pride does not elevate a man; it debases him. In God's eyes, it lowers a man to the level of a beast. But we will also discover that the Lord sends discipline for the purpose of raising man to godliness—and that path, ironically, leads first through humility.

∽ READING DANIEL 4:1–37 ∽

THE KING'S EDICT: *King Nebuchadnezzar sends out an official decree to his empire, explaining a dramatic change in his life. The change is evident even in the tone of his words.*

1. NEBUCHADNEZZAR THE KING: The events in this chapter took place sometime after Daniel's friends were saved from the fiery furnace, though it is not clear how much time elapsed between. This chapter encompasses an official edict that the king sent out to the people of Babylon.

To all peoples, nations, and languages: The edict was addressed in the same manner as Nebuchadnezzar's command to worship the image (3:4). This was probably a standard opening for official edicts, meaning "To all the subjects of King Nebuchadnezzar," yet it is still significant that the king was going back to the same audience he had once commanded to worship an idol. This time, however, he was telling them the truth about the one true God.

Peace be multiplied to you: Right from the beginning of the king's edict we notice a startling change in tone. In the previous chapter, Nebuchadnezzar had made a decree that "any people, nation, or language which speaks anything amiss against the God of Shadrach, Meshach, and Abed-Nego shall be cut in pieces, and their houses shall be made an ash heap; because there is no other God who can deliver like this" (Daniel 3:29). Now that same fiery king opened his edict with a greeting of peace.

2. the signs and wonders that the Most High God has worked for me: Here again we see a dramatic change from the king's previous understanding of God. Rather than referring to Him as "the God of Shadrach, Meshach, and Abed-Nego" (3:29), he now understood that He is "the Most High God," King of kings and Lord of lords. Perhaps more significantly, the king recognized that the Lord was working on his own behalf as well as for Daniel's friends, acknowledging, "Signs and wonders [have been] worked for me." Like Paul, King Nebuchadnezzar had gone from being a persecutor of God's people to one of God's people himself.

3. signs . . . wonders: Nebuchadnezzar was referring to the dramatic ways in which the Lord had made Himself known to the king, such as we saw in our previous study. God uses means both dramatic and subtle to reveal Himself to mankind, seeking to save the lost and teach all people about His character. The most complete demonstration of God's nature, of course, is contained within His Word, the Bible. The phrase should not be confused with the so-called Signs and Wonders Movement of modern times.

Another Dream: *Once again, the king has a strange dream and calls for his magicians and counselors—who of course fail to explain it adequately.*

4. at rest in my house, and flourishing in my palace: The Lord had made King Nebuchadnezzar very powerful and successful, but he had not recognized the source of that prosperity, thinking in his pride that he was somehow responsible. In this, he was like the man in Jesus' parable who thought his security lay in his possessions: "And I will say to my soul, 'Soul, you have many goods laid up for many years; take your ease; eat, drink, and be merry.' But God said to him, 'Fool! This night your soul will be required of you; then whose will those things be which you have provided?'" (Luke 12:19–20).

7. THE MAGICIANS, THE ASTROLOGERS, THE CHALDEANS, AND THE SOOTH-SAYERS: As happened in Study 2, Nebuchadnezzar had experienced a prophetic dream. He called in his usual group of so-called wise men—and once again they failed.

8. ACCORDING TO THE NAME OF MY GOD: That is, the god whom Nebuchadnezzar worshiped at that time, known as Bel-Merodach, an alternative form of Baal. His allegiance to that false god, however, was about to end.

9. NO SECRET TROUBLES YOU: Nebuchadnezzar had not yet come to understand that Daniel's gift of interpretation came directly from God, rather than from some innate ability he possessed.

10. A TREE: Nebuchadnezzar himself had compared Babylon to a spreading tree in building inscriptions.

11. ITS HEIGHT REACHED TO THE HEAVENS: Here is another echo of the Tower of Babel, "a tower whose top is in the heavens" (Genesis 11:4). Man's pride has led him to defy God since the early days of human history, and that trend is still prevalent today.

13. A WATCHER, A HOLY ONE: That is, an angel or messenger of God.

14. LET THE BEASTS GET OUT FROM UNDER IT: Since Nebuchadnezzar had refused to acknowledge God as the source of his authority, the Lord would remove him from his kingship. The beasts and birds in the dream represented the many peoples who were under the king's leadership; they would soon be taken out from under his dominion.

15. LEAVE THE STUMP AND ROOTS IN THE EARTH: The tree, as Daniel was about to explain, represented Nebuchadnezzar himself, who had grown so grand and proud in his kingly glory. The Lord was about to humble him in a most dramatic fashion, but He would not utterly destroy him. Fresh tree stumps generally put forth new growth if the roots are still healthy, and a new tree can grow up where an old one was cut down.. The iron and bronze band seem to suggest that the Lord would firmly protect the king from being utterly removed.

LET HIM GRAZE WITH THE BEASTS ON THE GRASS OF THE EARTH: This is a strange shift from the tree metaphor, suddenly changing to a person who would eat grass like a cow. Yet that is precisely what was about to happen to the king.

16. LET HIM BE GIVEN THE HEART OF A BEAST: This is a powerful insight into the true nature of man's pride. When a man elevates himself in his own mind, thinking that he is master of his own fate, he is actually debasing himself, making himself like a beast of the field. Paradoxically, it is a glory to man to recognize that he is completely dependent upon his Creator.

Let seven times pass over him: Daniel 7:25 uses this same term to mean years, so there is good reason to believe it means years here as well. Nebuchadnezzar would suffer his madness for a period of seven years.

17. the Most High rules in the kingdom of men: Here we have a central principle of these studies in a nutshell: God is the Supreme Ruler over all human affairs. What's more, we are told that God's chosen ruler is characterized by humility, not by pride. The good king understands that he rules only by the grace of God, and that He who raised up the king can also cast him down. In this sense, "the lowest of men" is the ruler who has a humble heart, turning constantly to God for guidance and wisdom.

Daniel's Interpretation: *The Lord once again gives Daniel the insight to interpret correctly what the king's dream means.*

---

19. Daniel . . . was astonished for a time: Daniel was astonished and troubled by the meaning of the dream, not by an inability to understand it. He was alarmed that the king was about to become like an ox of the field, and expressed a desire that it would be the fate of the king's enemies instead.

25. They shall drive you from men: The active voice ("they shall drive") might better be rendered in the passive voice here ("you shall be driven"). Nebuchadnezzar was being driven away not by people or angels but by God.

till you know that the Most High rules: The Lord made it clear to Nebuchadnezzar that his suffering was explicitly to teach him humility. The sooner he learned that lesson, the sooner his madness would pass.

27. break off your sins by being righteous: That is, act in a godly manner by repenting of your sinful pride and learning to be merciful. We have seen repeatedly throughout these studies that pride motivated King Nebuchadnezzar to a great degree, and his pride led him into frequent bursts of rage. Daniel respectfully begged the king to repent of those sins, allowing God to show mercy by sparing him the humiliation that was coming.

30. that I have built . . . by my mighty power: Here is the fundamental problem the Lord was addressing in Nebuchadnezzar's life. The king believed that his great success and power were due to his own efforts, and his grand building projects and political schemes were strictly "for the honor of my majesty." God did not figure into his plans simply because he had elevated himself to replace God in his thinking.

Nebuchadnezzar's Madness: *The Lord disciplines the king by letting him see the true nature of his own heart. In the end, however, the king is blessed.*

31. THE WORD WAS STILL IN THE KING'S MOUTH: Once again, compare the Lord's parable in Luke 12:19–20.

33. ATE GRASS LIKE OXEN: The Lord's discipline on Nebuchadnezzar was both appropriate and merciful. The king had raised himself in his own eyes to be equal with God, which is the most degrading and self-destructive thing a man can do, so it was fitting that he should find himself going about on all fours, eating grass like an ox. Nebuchadnezzar looked upon his kingdom and saw great splendor and beauty, but God looked upon the king's heart and saw ugly bestial qualities, which He made visible to the eyes of men as well. Yet this degradation was not to destroy Nebuchadnezzar but to humble him and cause him to repent.

34. I, NEBUCHADNEZZAR: You'll notice that this chapter begins and ends with the king speaking in the first person, while the period of his madness is described in the third person (v. 28–33), subtly underscoring his temporary loss of humanity.

LIFTED MY EYES TO HEAVEN: This was exactly what the Lord was trying to accomplish in the king's life. He had previously refused to look to God, looking instead upon himself and his accomplishments, so the Lord had caused him to become like a beast that can only look down at the grass it's eating. Yet as we've already mentioned, the Lord's goal was only to turn the king's eyes toward heaven; the moment he voluntarily did so, his reason returned and the Lord lifted His hand of discipline.

PRAISED AND HONORED HIM WHO LIVES FOREVER: Here at last King Nebuchadnezzar came to know the Lord as his God. No longer was He "the God of Shadrach, Meshach, and Abed-Nego" (3:29); instead, "Now I, Nebuchadnezzar, praise and extol and honor the King of heaven" (v. 37).

⌁ FIRST IMPRESSIONS ⌁

1. Why did Nebuchadnezzar tell the world about his humiliating madness? How is the tone of this chapter different from his words in previous chapters? What do these things reveal about the king's conversion?

2. What "signs and wonders" did the Lord give to King Nebuchadnezzar? Why? What work was He doing in the king's life?

3. *Why did the Lord send Nebuchadnezzar the dream of the tree? What was He trying to accomplish through that dream? How did Nebuchadnezzar respond to it?*

4. *How did pride influence Nebuchadnezzar's life? How did it affect his reign as king of Babylon? How did humility change him?*

Some Key Principles

Our security lies in God, not in our possessions or success.

King Nebuchadnezzar is remembered in history for his grand building projects and the prosperity of the Babylonian Empire under his leadership. He was the most powerful man in the world in his day, able to make or break any man with a simple word of command. He had constructed a magnificent hanging garden near his palace, to please his wife. It became one of the seven wonders of the ancient world. He constructed a massive network of walls and fortifications surrounding Babylon, some wide enough that several chariots could pass one another along the top. His own palace occupied some fifty acres of land, and he used kiln-baked bricks rather than sun-dried bricks on all his constructions to vastly increase their strength and longevity. When he stood atop his palace, he looked upon a magnificent city and told himself that he was lord of all he surveyed.

But he wasn't. No amount of military power could protect King Nebuchadnezzar from the sovereign hand of the Creator. What's more, no degree of glory and no brick-lined accomplishments could buy the king peace with God; only humility of spirit and obedience to His Word could accomplish that. This principle, of course, is equally true for all people, whether king or beggar. But the irony is that the king may well find it more difficult to obey than the beggar does, simply because the king has so much more of the world's trinkets. In this, Nebuchadnezzar demonstrated a weakness that is common to all men, thinking that his possessions and accomplishments could bring him lasting security.

Jesus warned of this danger in His parable of the rich fool who enjoyed great prosperity and fertile land. That farmer became complacent in his wealth, anticipating that he would enjoy many years of life free from worry or care. It was a fairly common mistake on his part to think that ample wealth and prosperity could bring him peace and safety, reflecting the way that most of the world thinks—"but God said to him, 'Fool! This night your soul will be required of you; then whose will those things be which you have provided?'" (Luke 12:20). The Lord calls His children to place their security in Him rather than in the things of this world, and to focus our efforts on growing in likeness to Christ. This is what Jesus called being "rich toward God" (Luke 12:21).

Pride debases a man, but humility lifts him up.

King Nebuchadnezzar was the most powerful man in the world, absolute sovereign over the Babylonian Empire. The world looked at him and saw a man who had enjoyed success in every venture, a man who had reached the pinnacle of human achievement. Then one day he suddenly went insane. His subjects watched aghast as he foraged through his royal garden, shuffling about on hands and knees, eating grass like a cow, his hair and nails grown filthy and unkempt, the rain and dew falling unheeded on his skin. How could such a great man be so suddenly debased?

But when God looked on Nebuchadnezzar, He did not see the pinnacle of humanity; He saw a man who had degraded his soul through pride and vanity. It was not a coincidence that the Lord chose to have the king go about on all fours; rather, He permitted the true nature of Nebuchadnezzar's pride to become evident to himself and the people around him. Pride is the sin of elevating oneself equal with God, and the paradoxical result is that it actually moves one *away* from God rather than toward Him. Mankind alone is made in the image of God, so any move away from God is also a move away from our intended human design—a move that makes us more like the beasts of the field.

"The fear of the LORD is to hate evil," wrote Solomon, describing God's perspective. "Pride and arrogance and the evil way and the perverse mouth I hate" (Proverbs 8:13). Proverbs 11:2 tells us that a prideful spirit brings shame to a man, but humility brings wisdom. "Pride goes before destruction, and a haughty spirit before a fall" (Proverbs 16:18). Nebuchadnezzar had to learn the lesson that "a man's pride will bring him low, but the humble in spirit will retain honor" (Proverbs 29:23).

Even the powerful must be humble to serve God.

Imagine if the president of the United States or the prime minister of England one day got out of bed, stripped off his clothes, and wandered outside on all fours! Picture a powerful world leader today wandering around the White House lawn on hands and knees, eating grass and grunting like a wild beast. Members of opposing political parties would call for that leader's immediate removal, and the world press would splash pictures and headlines on every front page and evening news report. It would be the end of that man's political career, and he would probably become a target of every comedian for generations to come.

God is not impressed by position or power. King Nebuchadnezzar was the leader of one of the most powerful empires in world history, and yet before he could serve God, he had to realize that he was a sinner in need of repentance. God does not save the powerful in a different way than he saves others. For anyone to turn to God, he must realize he has nothing that makes him worthy.

The author of Hebrews reminds us that "no chastening seems to be joyful for the present, but painful; nevertheless, afterward it yields the peaceable fruit of righteousness to those who have been trained by it" (Hebrews 12:11). Nebuchadnezzar's madness was certainly not pleasant while it lasted, but the result far outweighed the suffering he endured. The Lord struck the king with madness to bring him to an understanding of repentance. As Paul later wrote: "And we know that all things work together for good to those who love God, to those who are the called according to His purpose. For whom He foreknew, He also predestined to be conformed to the image of His Son, that He might be the firstborn among many brethren" (Romans 8:28–29).

⌁ DIGGING DEEPER ⌁

5. *Why did God cause Nebuchadnezzar to go mad? In what ways was his ailment an appropriate form of discipline for him? What did he learn from it?*

6. *Why did God reinstate Nebuchadnezzar as king after he humbled himself? Why did He not simply remove him, as He did with Belshazzar (Study 3)?*

7. Where do you tend to find your security? What defines your sense of success or failure in life? What is God's perspective on these matters?

8. Recall a time in your life when you were humiliated. What happened? How did you feel? What lessons did you learn from the experience?

⌁ TAKING IT PERSONALLY ⌁

9. Are you facing a time of discipline at present? What might the Lord be trying to teach you? How can you be an encouragement to someone else who is facing trials?

10. Make a list below of the blessings you enjoy. Take time this week to thank God for each of those blessings, reminding yourself that they are from Him and not the result of your own efforts.

8

QUEEN VASHTI AND QUEEN ESTHER

ESTHER 1–2

ᴧ CHARACTERS' BACKGROUND ᴧ

In 481 BC, King Ahasuerus (better known today as Xerxes) led his Persian forces in an invasion of Greece, hoping to increase his great empire. That campaign failed miserably, but its execution required a great deal of advance planning. Our study opens two years before that with a gathering of the king's nobles from all areas of his empire, which might well have been the planning session for that invasion. This gathering was a prolonged time of feasting and celebration, lasting a total of 180 days.

The events that concern us, however, occurred at the end of that time, when the king hosted another banquet, which lasted seven days. During the course of that feast, the king sent for his queen—hardly a dramatic moment on the surface. However, his reason for wanting her and his forceful tone made the queen uncomfortable, and she refused to appear. Suddenly a fairly commonplace event turned into a highly charged political confrontation, as the queen of Persia openly defied her king, and the implications became profound.

In this study, we will gain some behind-the-scenes insight into the royal relationship between the king and queen, and we will have the opportunity to assess the complementary roles God has made for men and women. We will also see striking contrasts between Queen Vashti and Esther, and between King Ahasuerus and Mordecai. In the process, we will learn that our actions matter to others around us, and godliness calls us to sobriety and humility.

ᴧ READING ESTHER 1:1–22 ᴧ

A ROYAL FEAST: *King Ahasuerus holds a banquet that lasts seven days, inviting everyone to attend, from the greatest to the least in his kingdom.*

1. IN THE DAYS OF AHASUERUS: The events of this section occurred around 483 BC, prior to Esther joining the king's household (Study 4).

FROM INDIA TO ETHIOPIA: The Persian Empire was huge by comparison with previous world powers. Its borders extended east to the Indus River (modern-day Pakistan) and west to Greece, extending south through Egypt into Ethiopia (modern-day Sudan, not modern Ethiopia) and north to the Caucasus Mountains.

2. SHUSHAN: Also known as Susa, today called Shush in Iran. The Persians actually had four capital cities, including Babylon, Ecbatana, and Persepolis.

3. IN THE THIRD YEAR OF HIS REIGN: Ahasuerus attempted to add Greece to the Persian Empire, which proved a disastrous failure. This gathering may well have been an extended planning session for that campaign.

5. A FEAST LASTING SEVEN DAYS: Weeklong feasts were not uncommon in the ancient world. Jewish wedding celebrations, for example, generally went on for a whole week.

7. THEY SERVED DRINKS IN GOLDEN VESSELS: The setting for this feast brings to mind the drunken debauch of King Belshazzar (Study 3). These golden vessels were not the sacred ones stolen from the Lord's temple in Jerusalem, of course, but the extravagance still suggests the king's pride.

8. THE DRINKING WAS NOT COMPULSORY: Persian custom dictated that all guests at a feast were to drink whenever the king raised his cup to his lips. It is possible that the king dispensed with that custom for diplomatic reasons, being sensitive to important members of his court who were from different cultures. It would have been important to build unity within his forces, if this feast was connected to his subsequent campaign against Greece.

9. QUEEN VASHTI: Her son Artaxerxes succeeded to the king's throne.

A DRUNKEN DEMAND: *The king grows "merry with wine" and demands that his queen present herself before his friends. But the queen refuses.*

10. THE HEART OF THE KING WAS MERRY WITH WINE: The Persians often drank heavily while making political decisions in the belief that drunkenness drew men closer to the gods.

11. IN ORDER TO SHOW HER BEAUTY TO THE PEOPLE: It is possible that the king was hoping to inspire some sort of patriotism in his followers prior to attacking Greece, but it is at least as likely that his drunkenness had impaired his judgment. One is reminded of Herod's drunken orgy in which a rash promise led to the beheading of John the Baptist (Mark 6).

12. BUT QUEEN VASHTI REFUSED TO COME: We are not told why the queen disobeyed the king's command, but she was most likely offended at being treated like a possession for the king to brag about.

THE KING WAS FURIOUS: We have seen angry kings repeatedly in these studies, and have noted that the anger of man does not work the righteousness of God. There is, however, another side to this issue.. The king's command may well have been arbitrary or even degrading, demanding that she be paraded before a room of drunken men.

13. THE WISE MEN WHO UNDERSTOOD THE TIMES: These would be the same types of counselors as those who were unable to advise either Nebuchadnezzar or Belteshazzar. King Ahasuerus apparently relied heavily on the advice of such worldly counselors, and his blind trust of Haman demonstrated a lack of wisdom in selecting them.

THE KING'S EDICT: *The king's counselors persuade him to make a law concerning his nation's marital relationships—and ending his own.*

17. THEY WILL DESPISE THEIR HUSBANDS: Judging from subsequent events with Haman, we might be safe in assuming that the counselors had ulterior motives in this advice, perhaps taking advantage of an opportunity to coerce the king into divorcing his queen. Yet the larger picture is important concerning Vashti: she was the queen, and as such her actions would become an example that others might follow. If the queen could defy her husband's authority with impunity, certainly the same would apply in ordinary marriages. After all, most men do not have the authority of the king.

18. THUS THERE WILL BE EXCESSIVE CONTEMPT AND WRATH: The sad truth is that neither king nor queen was functioning as a moral role model in this dispute. If women might follow the queen's example of defiance, then it is equally likely that ordinary men would imitate the king's example of rage.

19. SO THAT IT WILL NOT BE ALTERED: Once the king passed a law, it could never be repealed. This had dangerous results for the Jews, as we saw in Study 5, but we will also see in the next study that the Lord can override any of man's laws if He chooses—even those of the Persians.

VASHTI SHALL COME NO MORE BEFORE KING AHASUERUS: Ironically, Vashti got exactly what she demanded—and more so. She chose to remove herself from the king's presence when summoned, and ended up being denied access to his presence ever after.

ANOTHER WHO IS BETTER THAN SHE: This proved to be Esther, as we saw in Study 4.

20. ALL WIVES WILL HONOR THEIR HUSBANDS: It is good for a woman to honor her husband, but it is far better for her to do it out of obedience to God's Word rather

74

than through fear and compulsion. Husbands who imitate the love of Christ make it far easier for their wives to honor them.

⌒ READING ESTHER 2:8–11, 15–20 ⌒

THE BETTER WOMAN: *The king's counselors urge him to find a woman who is better than Vashti. That woman turns out to be Esther.*

8. ESTHER ALSO WAS TAKEN: It is impossible to tell if Esther went into this forced marriage voluntarily or against her will. Regardless, she presents a contrast to Vashti, who refused to go.

9. SHE OBTAINED HIS FAVOR: It is worth noting how frequently this phrase appears concerning Esther. She found favor with all who were in authority because of God's providential control of her life, seen through her submissive spirit.

10. MORDECAI HAD CHARGED HER NOT TO REVEAL IT: Esther refrained from revealing that she was a Jew simply because Mordecai told her not to. Yet Mordecai was her cousin, not her husband—and certainly not the king! She chose to submit to his counsel, while Vashti defied the authority of both husband and king. This also illustrates how dangerous it was to be a Jew in those days.

11. EVERY DAY MORDECAI PACED IN FRONT OF THE COURT: Mordecai did not hesitate to take the lead in his family, yet he made it easier for Esther to honor his authority by loving her in a careful, godly fashion, seeking her welfare at all times and at cost to himself.

15. SHE REQUESTED NOTHING: As mentioned previously, Esther demonstrated a deep respect for the wisdom of those in authority over her. Her willing submission and readiness to accept advice in turn brought her the respect of others.

17. THE KING LOVED ESTHER: We have considered the fact that God's sovereign hand was at work in this debasing situation. God gave Esther favor in the king's eyes because it was part of His plan.

19. MORDECAI SAT WITHIN THE KING'S GATE: Once again we find Mordecai hovering nearby out of his deep concern for Esther's welfare.

20. ESTHER OBEYED THE COMMAND OF MORDECAI: This is a striking statement. Esther was now married and no longer under the domestic authority of her cousin. What's more, she was now the queen of Persia! Yet she still chose to honor Mordecai for his wisdom and godliness by humbling herself and following his advice.

⌁ First Impressions ⌁

1. How did the king's drunkenness influence the events in this chapter? How might things have been different if he'd remained sober through this narrative?

2. Why did King Ahasuerus command his wife's appearance at the feast? What reasons might she have had for refusing?

3. If you'd been in Vashti's position, how would you have responded to the king's command?

4. How does King Ahasuerus contrast with Mordecai in this study? How does Esther contrast with Vashti?

⌁ Some Key Principles ⌁

Drunkenness leads to foolishness.

The Persians believed that alcoholic spirits would make them more attuned to the spiritual world, giving them wisdom in decisions. King Ahasuerus, however, demonstrated the foolishness of such a notion when he drank too much wine at his grand banquet. The wine did influence his decision-making ability, but not in the direction of wisdom. It is doubly ironic that he evidently recognized the dangers of drunkenness when he gave his guests the freedom to remain sober.

Drunkenness affects more than a person's physical being; it influences one's spirit as well. For example, alcohol is notorious for "lowering a person's inhibitions," which is merely another way of saying that it hinders one's ability to resist temptations. And resisting temptation is a spiritual issue, not a physical concern.

The New Testament teaches that drunkenness leads a person to ignore the promptings of God's Holy Spirit, causing him to obey the promptings of the flesh instead. The best solution to drunkenness, therefore, is to be filled with the Spirit, as Paul commanded: "And do not be drunk with wine, in which is dissipation; but be filled with the Spirit, speaking to one another in psalms and hymns and spiritual songs, singing and making melody in your heart to the Lord, giving thanks always for all things to God the Father in the name of our Lord Jesus Christ, submitting to one another in the fear of God" (Ephesians 5:18–21). A Christian becomes the temple of the Holy Spirit (1 Corinthians 3:16), and that temple should be filled with God's Spirit rather than intoxicating spirits.

Provoking others leads to wrath.

Queen Vashti did have legitimate reason for resenting the king's summons to his banquet. She probably felt that she was being used as a political tool or a prized possession, and being paraded before a room of leering men would be degrading and offensive to any woman—and Vashti was a queen! Rather than being highly concerned with his wife's welfare and virtue, the king felt no qualms about exposing her to the eyes of strangers. No wonder the queen was not pleased with the command.

Nevertheless, the queen's response was not wise. Her husband's command certainly risked humiliating her, but that did not excuse her for publicly humiliating him in return. Furthermore, Ahasuerus was the king, which means her defiant response was against a God-ordained authority. Proverbs rightly warns, "The wrath of a king is like the roaring of a lion; whoever provokes him to anger sins against his own life. It is honorable for a man to stop striving, since any fool can start a quarrel" (Proverbs 20:2–3).

Daniel and his friends demonstrated this principle back in Study 1 when they gently offered an alternative to the king's command concerning forbidden foods. They were able to avoid disobeying God's commands while also not provoking the king to wrath. Paul pointed out that the root of provocation is pride, the idea that my desires are more important than someone else's. He offered the better approach: "But the fruit of the Spirit is love, joy, peace, longsuffering, kindness, goodness, faithfulness, gentleness, self-control. Against such there is no law. And those who are Christ's have crucified the flesh with its passions and desires. If we live in the Spirit, let us also walk in the Spirit. Let us not become conceited, provoking one another, envying one another" (Galatians 5:22–26).

God desires that men and women observe their God-given roles.

The interactions between King Ahasuerus and Queen Vashti in this study present a poor example of marital relations. The king commanded his wife the way a tyrant would command a lowly slave, exercising a lordly authority that expected to be obeyed without question. To make things worse, his command was very degrading to a woman (to say nothing of a queen), insisting she parade herself before a gathering of strangers so that they might be impressed with her husband's good fortune.

Yet modern readers should resist the temptation of forcing twenty-first-century Western sensibilities into the text. We understand that Adam was created before Eve and that Adam named her, which demonstrated his God-given authority over Eve (Genesis 2:21–24; 1 Timothy 2:11–15; 1 Corinthians 11:7–12). We must not allow this bad example of King Ahasuerus and Queen Vashti to persuade us that the concept of male headship is no longer viable in today's world. God instituted a hierarchy of authority at the time of creation, and the principles He established then are still completely applicable today. God gave Adam headship over Eve, holding him responsible for her spiritual well-being.

There are, of course, two sides to this controversial coin, and the flip side is that God commands husbands to love their wives as Christ loved the church—which is a very tall order indeed. Paul summed up these roles: "Wives, submit to your own husbands, as to the Lord. For the husband is head of the wife, as also Christ is head of the church; and He is the Savior of the body. Therefore, just as the church is subject to Christ, so let the wives be to their own husbands in everything. Husbands, love your wives, just as Christ also loved the church and gave Himself for her. . . . So husbands ought to love their own wives as their own bodies; he who loves his wife loves himself. . . . Nevertheless let each one of you in particular so love his own wife as himself, and let the wife see that she respects her husband" (Ephesians 5:22–25, 28, 33).

⤳ Digging Deeper ⤳

5. How might the events of Esther 1 have been different if the king and queen had a godly marriage? How would that compare with the king's edict to the men and women of his kingdom?

6. What influence might the king's actions have on the men of his kingdom? What influence might Vashti's actions have on the women? How might their influences have been different if their actions had been godly?

7. How did the king's brazen drunkenness influence those around him? Even though the king allowed his subjects to refrain from drinking, which were his subjects more likely to follow: his words or his actions?

8. When have you provoked someone to anger with your words or deeds? How might things have ended differently if you'd behaved differently?

⤳ Taking It Personally ⤳

9. Why does God's Word teach that men are to be the spiritual authority in marriage and by extension the church (cf. 1 Timothy 2:11–14)? How well are you following that model?

10. Look back at low points of sin in your life. How was God at work at those times in your life? What good did He bring about?

9

MORDECAI

⌁ CHARACTER'S BACKGROUND ⌁

Esther's cousin Mordecai was "the son of Jair, the son of Shimei, the son of Kish, a Benjamite," as we will learn in this study. Great-granddad Kish evidently was living in Judah at the time that Nebuchadnezzar carried the Jews into Babylonian captivity, joining Daniel and his friends there. After Babylon fell to the Medo-Persians (Study 3), the Jews were further scattered about the Persian Empire. Mordecai's family settled in Susa, one of the four capitals of that empire.

In this study, however, Mordecai's ancestors will play a greater role than meets the eye, for he was probably descended from King Saul. You will remember that the Lord had commanded King Saul to wipe out the Amalekites, but he had not fully obeyed (see Study 5). He had allowed the Amalekite king, Agag, to remain alive, and one of that king's descendants was living in Susa along with Mordecai—Haman, the enemy of the Jews. In this study, we will see how that ancient conflict came to a head. We will also learn some important aspects of a godly character, as demonstrated in the life of Mordecai, and contrasted in the character of Haman.

⌁ READING ESTHER 2:21–23 ⌁

AN ASSASSINATION PLOT: *Mordecai uncovers an assassination plot, and he saves the king's life. His reward, however, is to be forgotten, but only for a time.*

21. IN THOSE DAYS: We are now back to the time when Esther had just been made queen, around 479 BC.

MORDECAI SAT WITHIN THE KING'S GATE: The gate to a city was important on many levels. City officials would sit there to conduct official business and to pass judgment on civil cases, much the way that modern courthouses and city halls function. Mordecai's presence there indicates that he held an important position in the king's service, perhaps as a result of Esther's influence as queen.

DOORKEEPERS: These two men evidently held positions of some trust in the king's court, and might have been members of his personal bodyguard. They were undoubtedly in a position to assassinate the king—a fate that befell many ancient monarchs.

22. THE MATTER BECAME KNOWN TO MORDECAI: Mordecai's job at the king's gate placed him in a situation where he could easily gather information. His action of informing the king through Esther indicated a strong loyalty to those in authority over him. It would have been far easier to tell himself that it was none of his concern.

23. HANGED ON A GALLOWS: The Persians actually executed criminals by impalement, and it is likely that they were the inventors of crucifixion. They probably impaled these men, then hanged their corpses on a gallows as a public display of what would befall any who sought the king's harm. Haman's sons later suffered a similar fate.

IT WAS WRITTEN IN THE BOOK OF THE CHRONICLES: But nothing further was done to reward Mordecai. It is interesting that there is no indication that Mordecai expected any reward.

⌁ READING ESTHER 3:1–7 ⌁

BOWING BEFORE HAMAN: *The king orders all his subjects to pay homage to Haman, but there is one man in the city who refuses: Mordecai. This fills Haman with vengeful wrath.*

1. HAMAN . . . THE AGAGITE: We learned about Haman's ancestry in Study 5, and about King Agag and the Amalekites, whom King Saul had been commanded to kill. It is important now to know that Mordecai was descended from King Saul.

SET HIS SEAT ABOVE ALL THE PRINCES: We are not told why Haman was honored in this fashion, but the author may have deliberately omitted any reason in order to increase the contrast between Haman, the undeserving recipient of honor, and Mordecai, the unrecognized hero.

2. MORDECAI WOULD NOT BOW OR PAY HOMAGE: God's law forbade His people to bow themselves in worship before idols (Exodus 20:4–6), but that might not have been the reason for Mordecai's refusal here. Ancient historians wrote that Persian court etiquette required a person to bow to his superiors as an act of respect, not worship, and the Jews themselves would sometimes bow before kings (1 Samuel 24:8). It seems more likely that Mordecai remembered the Lord's command concerning the Amalekites: "You will blot out the remembrance of Amalek from under heaven. You shall not forget" (Deuteronomy 25:19). Whatever his motivation, Mordecai's refusal to bow was based on his commitment to God's Word and God's people.

4. Mordecai had told them that he was a Jew: It seems odd that Mordecai would not follow the advice he had given Esther (2:10), but he was probably forced to reveal his Jewish identity as the reason for his refusal to bow before Haman.

5. Haman was filled with wrath: The wrath of men is a recurring theme in these studies, and once again we see that it does not lead toward God's righteousness. Notice that Haman had the respect of nearly everyone in the empire, but could not get over the fact that one man refused to bow to him.

6. Haman sought to destroy all the Jews: Mordecai had not forgotten God's commands concerning the Amalekites, but neither had Haman. He nursed an ancient resentment toward the people of God from an event that had occurred more than five hundred years earlier.

7. they cast Pur: The Persians would cast lots, which they called Pur, to determine the "will of the gods" they served. This would be similar to tossing modern dice to make a decision. From the Persian word *Pur*, the Jews named their celebration of *Purim* to commemorate the events of this book.

⌁ Reading Esther 4:1–8 ⌁

Sackcloth and Ashes: *Mordecai learns of Haman's scheme to annihilate the Jews, and he is filled with grief. Queen Esther, however, has not yet learned of the plot.*

1. all that had happened: That is, Haman's wicked decree had been signed by the king's ring, condemning the Jews to slaughter (as we saw in Study 5).

sackcloth and ashes: Sackcloth was a coarse material used in sacking, comparable to burlap. Wearing sackcloth, tearing clothes, and covering the head with ash was an outward sign of deep mourning and grief. Mordecai certainly was grieving over the wicked decree, but he might also have been feeling that he had personally brought it upon the Jews. But Haman's wrath had been kindled by Mordecai's obedience to God's Word, and the Lord was using these events to unfold His plan.

2. the king's gate: Mordecai's official position in the king's court involved sitting in the king's gate (2:19), the place where much official business was conducted on a daily basis. A person in sackcloth would have been unseemly in such a place, like a beggar wandering into the king's court. Mordecai's open lamentations were placing him at risk, as he could not carry out his duties inside the gate.

4. SHE SENT GARMENTS TO CLOTHE MORDECAI: Esther did not know about Haman's decree at this point, and was puzzled over what was happening to her cousin. She may have wanted Mordecai to remove his sackcloth so that she could have better access to him, although the Persian prohibitions against men speaking with royal women make that seem less likely. It is also possible that she was trying to encourage him, suggesting that whatever was wrong could be put right with her influence. But Mordecai refused to accept them because the situation would not be resolved through political influence, only through the sovereign hand of God.

8. THAT HE MIGHT COMMAND HER TO GO IN TO THE KING: As we have noted previously, it seems strange that Mordecai would issue a command to the queen, yet it does present an interesting parallel to our last study, where we saw the king command Queen Vashti to enter his presence for his own pleasure. Here we have Mordecai, with no kingly authority, command the queen to enter the king's presence in order to plead for the lives of her people.

⌒ READING ESTHER 5:9–14 ⌒

BUILD THE GALLOWS HIGH: *Haman's joy is marred by the existence of Mordecai, so his family suggests that he have the Jew hanged. Haman builds his own gallows.*

9. JOYFUL AND WITH A GLAD HEART: Esther had just requested that the king and Haman attend a banquet in their honor, as we saw in Study 4. It is interesting to see that such great rejoicing could be instantly nullified by the mere sight of Mordecai refusing to "stand or tremble before him." This demonstrates the all-consuming hatred Haman had toward God's people, as well as the shallowness and vanity of his own character. The fact that Mordecai was back at the king's gate also indicates that he had removed the sackcloth and resumed normal clothing. This and his refusal to tremble in the presence of the one who had decreed his death demonstrate the depth of Mordecai's faith: he knew the Lord would deliver His people.

11. TOLD THEM OF HIS GREAT RICHES: Again we are reminded of the Lord's parable of the rich fool (Luke 12:1–21). Haman's boasting presupposed that all his blessings had come to him through his own merit—even though no merit was mentioned for his promotion in the king's service.

14. THAT MORDECAI BE HANGED ON IT: This scheme probably involved impaling Mordecai, then hanging his body for display, as befell the two eunuchs in chapter 2.

THE WHEEL TURNS: *The king has insomnia, Haman arrives at court at the right moment, and other tiny details reveal God's sovereign hand.*

1. THE KING COULD NOT SLEEP: Here once again we witness the amazing sovereignty of God over the smallest details of men's affairs. On the very night that Haman was building a gallows for Mordecai, the king happened to suffer from insomnia. And his solution to that problem? Read from the book that chronicled an assassination attempt, of course! (That attempt had probably occurred some five years earlier.) The human perspective would see these as amazing coincidences, but God's Word demonstrates that it was no accident—it was part of God's deliberate plan. There are no coincidences or surprises under His sovereign hand.

3. NOTHING HAS BEEN DONE FOR HIM: The world's system is often unjust, rewarding the unworthy (like Haman) while ignoring those who deserve honor. But the Lord is the "rewarder of those who diligently seek Him" (Hebrews 11:6).

4. HAMAN HAD JUST ENTERED: Yet again we see the perfect sovereignty of God at work, causing Haman to enter the king's court at the exact moment He chose.

TO SUGGEST THAT THE KING HANG MORDECAI: God's sovereignty is never hindered by man's intentions. People make choices between good and evil, and the Lord uses those choices to further His own plans—including the evil choices. The Lord was able to use even Haman's wicked scheme to further His purposes, but the wicked eventually find their own plans lashing back against themselves.

6. THE MAN WHOM THE KING DELIGHTS TO HONOR: Haman presents a stark contrast to Mordecai once again. Mordecai had done the king a service without expecting any reward, while Haman thought only of his own advancement at all times—even when he had done nothing to warrant it. Just as the Lord rewards the righteous, He also rewards wickedness with its own fruit in due season.

9. PARADE HIM ON HORSEBACK THROUGH THE CITY SQUARE: Haman's greedy suggestion was that the honored man should be treated as though equal with the king himself. Of course, he thought that honor was coming his way. To parade through the streets on a royal horse, wearing the king's own robes, would have told the people of the city that the honored man was to be obeyed with the same authority as the king.

10. DO SO FOR MORDECAI THE JEW: The sudden and ironic reversal of fortune in this history is worthy of great literature, something that a writer like Shakespeare might have invented. But these events are true, not a work of fiction. The Lord allowed Haman's perversity to define and engineer his own humiliation.

12. Mordecai went back to the king's gate. . . . Haman hurried to his house: Here is another interesting contrast between these two antagonists. When Haman had been honored and elevated, he went home and threw a party to celebrate, boasting grossly before family and friends about his great accomplishments. But after Mordecai was honored and elevated, he immediately went back to work. He had earned his preferment, in contrast to Haman, and he demonstrated the quality of his character by not letting it go to his head, continuing to diligently serve the king as he had always done.

13. before whom you have begun to fall: We saw the remainder of Haman's life in Study 5. His determination to rise in life led to his downfall, while Mordecai's patient trust in God's sovereignty led to a lasting and good reward.

∽ First Impressions ∽

1. If you had been in Mordecai's position, what would you have done upon learning of an assassination plot? How would you have felt in the same situation if no reward followed?

2. Why was Haman so angry at Mordecai? What does this reveal about what kind of person Haman was?

3. Compare and contrast Haman and Mordecai. What similarities were there in their lives? How were their characters different?

4. *What evidences can you see in these passages of God's sovereign control? How might you have viewed those events if you'd been living through them at the time?*

∿ Some Key Principles ∿

Do not forget God's commands.

Mordecai's refusal to bow before Haman might appear at first to be stubborn pride, but that was not typical of his character. He was devoted to the king's service and diligent in his work. His refusal to bow was motivated by his commitment to the Word of God, like Daniel's concern regarding the king's diet. The Lord had commanded His people to not forget the sins of the Amalekites or His judgment against that nation (Deuteronomy 25:19), and Mordecai was "remembering to remember."

Remembering God's Word requires a deliberate choice on our part, because forgetting His commands is an inherent part of our fallen sinful nature. This is the reason that the Lord stressed the importance of remembering His Word, commanding His people, "Only take heed to yourself, and diligently keep yourself, lest you forget the things your eyes have seen, and lest they depart from your heart all the days of your life. And teach them to your children and your grandchildren" (Deuteronomy 4:9). The Lord further warned His people that forgetting His Word would lead them to say in their hearts, "My power and the might of my hand have gained me this wealth" (Deuteronomy 8:17)—the very sin Haman committed.

God's commands to "take heed" and "diligently keep yourself" demonstrate that remembering His Word requires ongoing effort on our part. Taking heed involves paying attention to one's actions and attitudes, constantly double-checking them against the Scriptures. Keeping oneself diligently requires daily time in the Lord's presence, confessing sins and seeking His guidance. It is through such daily disciplines, coupled with the indwelling power of the Holy Spirit, that God's people remember to remember.

We are responsible for obedience; God is responsible for what follows.

Mordecai obeyed God's commands with diligence. He was faithful to carry out his duties at the king's gate; in fact, nearly every time he's mentioned in these studies, that's where we find him. Dealing with secret plots against the king's life probably did not fall into his basic job description, yet he understood that he had an obligation before the Lord to protect the king and reveal that plot. He reported it to the queen, not with an eye to being rewarded by the king, but because he knew it was the right thing to do. He obeyed God, and left the consequences in His hands.

Mordecai also obeyed the Lord's Word by not bowing before Haman, and he did so knowing that he was making a very powerful enemy—but he obeyed just the same. This attitude lay at the root of his admonition to Esther to approach the king on behalf of the Jews, even at risk of her own life; "Yet who knows," he reminded her, "whether you have come to the kingdom for such a time as this?" (Esther 4:14). Obey the Lord, he advised, and leave the consequences in His hands.

It is important to remember that Mordecai and Esther did not know the end of the story the way we do; they were actually living out the events, and there was no guarantee they would live to see tomorrow. Like Daniel's three friends in the fiery furnace, they were called upon to obey the Lord without being told what consequences would follow. The same is true for Christians today: our job is to obey God's Word while trusting Him for the outcome. The good news is that He has not changed since Mordecai's day; as He was faithful to His people then, so He will prove faithful today and tomorrow.

Anger is often driven by lack of perspective.

There is a rich irony in the fate of Haman, a man whose life was characterized by self-promotion and boasting. Haman had everything he could want, and nearly every person in the entire empire bowed before him. But he did not enjoy those blessings because he was so fixated on the one person who did not honor him. Haman's high self-regard made him blind to the notion that there might be others more worthy of honor than he, and his suggestion to the king reflected the extent of his own over-reaching greed and covetousness. J. Vernon McGee used to say, "You can tell the size of a man by the size of the things that make him angry." Haman was an immature person who refused to see his own blessings because he was blinded by his own pride.

In a loose way, we Christians can see ourselves in Haman. We have been given everything important; our sins have been forgiven, we have access to God through prayer, and we get to go to heaven when we die. God has given us a mission to evangelize others, and has given us His Spirit to accomplish that task. We have everything we could ever need, yet like Haman we often fail to see that, and instead get angry at inconsequential events.

The Christian can be angry at sin, and anger at the rejection of the Lord is certainly understandable. But the reality is that the Christian has no reason to be angry when he is slighted. We do not love our own honor, but rather we care deeply about the honor of the Lord. Jesus, as our example, was filled with zeal for His Father's house (John 2:17), but turned the other cheek when He was wrongly attacked (John 19:2). Remembering the glories of God and our riches in Christ should keep us from being angry at the wrong things.

↳ Digging Deeper ↲

5. *If you had been in Mordecai's position, how would you have felt while being paraded around on the king's horse? How might it have affected your life long-term?*

6. *If you had been in Haman's position, how would you have handled your sudden elevation to the king's right hand? How would you have reacted to someone who refused to bow before you?*

7. When have you been able to see some of God's reason for times of hardship in your life? When have you not been able to see His reason? What role does faith play in the process?

8. What steps do you take on a regular basis to "remember to remember" God's Word? What other disciplines might be helpful (Scripture memorization, daily Bible reading, in-depth Bible study, etc.)?

⤳ Taking It Personally ⤳

9. How do you generally respond to a person who thinks he's superior to you? When do you tend to treat others that way? What will you do this week to learn to treat others as better than yourself?

10. What areas of your life at present require faith? What will you do this week to increase your faith in God's sovereignty over those areas?

Section 3:

Themes

In This Section:

10

STANDING BOLDLY FOR GOD

DANIEL 6

⋏ THEMATIC BACKGROUND ⋏

Throughout these studies, we have met godly men and women who have found themselves in a wide variety of difficult circumstances, situations in which their very lives were at stake. Some of these situations were beyond the control of the individuals, but not all of them. Esther and Mordecai had no control over Haman's edict; that danger was thrust upon them by the actions of someone else. Daniel's three friends, on the other hand, did have some control over the outcome of their situation: they could have neutralized the danger by choosing to bow before the king's statue.

In this study, we will see Daniel face a situation very similar to that of his friends in Study 6. In this case, however, the circumstances were very personal, as the king's edict was engineered specifically to bring harm to Daniel. Like his friends, he could have avoided the danger with a small compromise—simply being more secretive about his faith and not openly praying to the Lord. We will discover, however, that Daniel was not ashamed of his faith and not afraid to let others see it. His boldness meant that he would have to face the death penalty, but in the end his testimony had an impact on the entire Persian Empire.

⋏ READING DANIEL 6:1–28 ⋏

AN EXCELLENT SPIRIT: *Daniel is now in his eighties, but we find him faithfully serving another king. And this king, like others, recognizes his excellent spirit.*

1. DARIUS: This is Darius the Mede, who took the kingdom of Babylon away from Belshazzar (Study 3). Nothing is known about him apart from Daniel's account.

2. THREE GOVERNORS: Darius had three men who shared the responsibilities of being second-in-command over the kingdom. Their primary duties were to prevent any rebellion against the king and to oversee taxes and other national financial matters. Belshazzar had named Daniel "the third ruler in the kingdom" of Babylon

(Daniel 5:29), a defunct empire, but the Lord had placed him even higher in Babylon's successor.

3. DANIEL DISTINGUISHED HIMSELF: Daniel was probably in his eighties by this time, and a lifetime of diligence and faithfulness, coupled with the Lord's faithful blessings, caused him to excel in whatever job he was given.

AN EXCELLENT SPIRIT WAS IN HIM: This refers to Daniel's attitude and character, his servant's heart and faithfulness both to God and king. Yet we must also recognize that the Spirit of God was at work in his life, giving him wisdom and blessing his work.

THE KING GAVE THOUGHT TO SETTING HIM OVER THE WHOLE REALM: Pharaoh had done this for Joseph (Genesis 41), lifting him out of a dungeon pit and setting him on the throne. The process for Daniel would prove to be different, however.

LOOKING FOR TROUBLE: *The other governors and their subordinates become jealous of Daniel's favored status with the king, and diligently look for a way to remove him.*

4. SOUGHT TO FIND SOME CHARGE AGAINST DANIEL: It is important to recognize that Daniel's enemies were the most powerful men in the kingdom, second only to the king himself. He was completely outnumbered as well, since two of the three governors turned against him. They were motivated by pure envy, jealous of Daniel's possible promotion above them.

THEY COULD FIND NO CHARGE OR FAULT: Daniel's diligence and faithfulness set him above reproach such that even his enemies could not find anything to fault him with, though they tried hard to do so. Yet even this does not guarantee that a godly person will never suffer injustice.

5. CONCERNING THE LAW OF HIS GOD: Here is another sad irony in the thinking of the world. Daniel's enemies could not find any wrongdoing in his life, so they concluded that his faith in God was his one weak point! The world sees faith in and obedience to God's Word as a weakness, as though it were saner to place one's faith in the learning of men, or what we call science. But when a nation sets out to defy God, the end result is to outlaw righteousness.

6. THRONGED BEFORE THE KING: The Hebrew verb here literally means "to come thronging in a tumultuous manner." It suggests an unruly mob rushing upon the king in loud indignation. These enemies of Daniel had no legitimate grievance against him, so they made up for it in loud bluster. One is reminded of the artificial outrage of people today who take offense at the Word of God, manufacturing all sorts of rules concerning what is deemed politically correct in words, deeds, and beliefs.

7. ALL THE GOVERNORS OF THE KINGDOM: This, of course, was a lie, since Daniel had not endorsed such a proposal, but it is ever the tactic of the world to claim that "everybody does it" or "all the experts agree" concerning false teaching. And even if such claims *were* true, God's will is still not determined by vote.

AN EVIL DECREE: *Daniel's enemies persuade the king to force all people to worship him—and in the process they make themselves God's enemies too.*

WHOEVER PETITIONS ANY GOD OR MAN: This decree was worded carefully. On the surface, it did not seem to have any religious significance; after all, one can petition a king or a judge or a town council. Americans today are very familiar with the process of signing a petition, and it does not involve any element of religious devotion. But below the surface of the decree lay the idea that King Darius was a god—indeed, he was portrayed as the only true God, the only one to whom any man might pray. (The notion of such supreme deity lasting only thirty days is rather ludicrous, of course, but a man who succumbs to the notion that he is God is unlikely to quibble over details.) Another subtlety lay in the fact that no particular deity was singled out; all gods other than Darius were forbidden. Daniel's enemies were God's enemies, striving to outlaw His followers from worshiping Him by clothing it under the guise of neutrality and fairness.

THE DEN OF LIONS: Ancient kings in the Middle East considered lion hunting a pastime suitable for royalty, much as fox hunting was in Britain at one time. Thus, King Darius might well have a supply of lions on hand for his own sport, perhaps even breeding them for that purpose. The den was actually a pit in the ground with a narrow opening at the top to permit food to be dropped in without the lions escaping. (There probably was another caged door leading into the pit to get the animals in and out.) Kings (and later Roman emperors) would utilize these captive beasts to dispose of political enemies.

8. IT CANNOT BE CHANGED: We have already seen that Persian laws could not be repealed once they were enacted by the king.

DANIEL'S SOLUTION: *Daniel responds to the dangerous situation by going home and getting on his knees. What he prays may surprise you.*

---

10. HE WENT HOME: Daniel's immediate reaction upon hearing the king's dreadful decree was to go home and pray. It is important to understand that opening his windows was his regular practice. He was not trying to openly flaunt his disobedience to the king's decree, but he was also not allowing the decree to change his daily prayer habits. Daniel may have been consciously following the pattern of prayer that Solomon had set forth hundreds of years earlier (2 Chronicles 6:38–39), and which David practiced (Psalm 55:17).

PRAYED AND GAVE THANKS: Here is a surprising element in Daniel's prayer. We might have expected him to grieve and lament before the Lord, much as Mordecai did upon learning of Haman's plot. But Daniel prayed and gave thanks. We are not told what specifically he was thankful for, but we can safely assume that his thanks were motivated by a complete faith in God's sovereign and faithful care of His people. The Lord calls His people to be characterized by a thankful heart (Ephesians 5:20). This does not preclude intercession for others and making requests for our own needs, however, and Daniel's prayer included supplication for the Lord's deliverance (v. 11).

13. ONE OF THE CAPTIVES FROM JUDAH: Daniel lived in Babylon for more than sixty years, and he held one of the highest offices in the empire. Yet his enemies deliberately described him in these words to degrade him in the mind of the king, laying the seed of suspicion that Daniel might be planning some form of rebellion.

14. THE KING . . . WAS GREATLY DISPLEASED WITH HIMSELF: The king had seen himself as a god, but in one swift moment saw the truth about himself—and he was ashamed. This, however, is the first step toward salvation.

HE LABORED . . . TO DELIVER HIM: This is a strong testimony to the character of Daniel. The king recognized his value to his rule, and evidently also cared for him as an individual.

16. YOUR GOD, WHOM YOU SERVE CONTINUALLY: What a powerful statement of Daniel's faithful testimony! Everyone around him knew that he served the Lord, and did so continually, and that testimony was bearing fruit—although potentially at cost of Daniel's life. It is significant that the king expressed such a profound faith in God's ability and willingness to preserve Daniel from the lions, a faith that was influenced by Daniel's testimony.

***

THE DEN OF LIONS: *Daniel is thrown into the lions' den, just as his friends had been thrown into a fiery furnace. Once again, God's power and faithfulness are shown forth.*

17. A STONE WAS BROUGHT: The stone was laid across the opening in order to prevent anyone from rescuing Daniel from the lions, and the seals were affixed to ensure that the stone was not moved. This episode in Daniel's life also painted a striking picture of the resurrection of Christ, whose tomb was sealed by Pilate lest the disciples should steal His body (Matthew 27:66). Unlike Daniel, however, Jesus did die—yet no stone could keep Him in the tomb!

18. SPENT THE NIGHT FASTING: Darius's repentance seems to have been genuine, and he may well have spent the night praying for Daniel's deliverance, in spite of his limited understanding of God.

20. HAS YOUR GOD . . . BEEN ABLE TO DELIVER YOU: The king's knowledge of God's character was incomplete, but Daniel's deliverance would demonstrate conclusively that He does indeed have the power to save. He has more than just the power, in fact; He takes pleasure in caring for those who serve Him. Daniel's faithful testimony and God's faithful character combined in this episode to teach the king that there is only one true God, the Creator of heaven and earth.

21. O KING, LIVE FOREVER: This was a standard form of addressing a king in Daniel's time, yet it was also a very appropriate thing for Daniel to say. He wanted the king to gain eternal life through faith in God—the only way that such a wish could come to fulfillment.

22. I WAS FOUND INNOCENT BEFORE HIM: What a tremendously glorious thing to be able to say! Yet every Christian can say the same, because God sees us through the blood of His Son, Jesus. No person can ever say that he or she is innocent of sin, yet God will one day declare each Christian to be so, because Jesus paid the debt on the cross (Isaiah 53:6; Romans 3:23).

23. THE KING WAS EXCEEDINGLY GLAD: Other kings we have met in these studies have responded in rage, but Darius responded with joy and gladness. His focus evidently was on saving Daniel rather than on avenging his enemies. It brought him delight to discover the nature of God's grace and salvation.

NO INJURY WHATEVER WAS FOUND ON HIM: Daniel's friends were unharmed by fire, and Daniel was unharmed by roaring lions. The temporal world cannot harm God's people without His permission.

BECAUSE HE BELIEVED IN HIS GOD: It was Daniel's faith that permitted God's salvation to be shown forth (Ephesians 2:8–9).

24. THEM, THEIR CHILDREN, AND THEIR WIVES: Persian law held that a man's entire family shared in his guilt, as we saw in the case of Haman (Esther 9:25). The Lord commanded the same fate to Achan and his family (Joshua 7:20–26).

THE LIONS OVERPOWERED THEM: This demonstrated that the lions were in fact ferocious and hungry, lest anyone attempt to refute God's power in Daniel's salvation. Even today, skeptics attempt to refute the resurrection of Christ in similar ways, claiming that Jesus only "swooned" on the cross but did not die—yet the facts of His death and resurrection are irrefutable.

25. Peace be multiplied to you: Nebuchadnezzar used similar words to open his own decree of conversion to faith in the one true God. Again, we see a king expressing peace rather than wrath upon coming to understand the character of God.

26. He is the living God: King Darius referred to the Lord as "the God of Daniel," rather than his own God, yet his conversion would seem to have been genuine just the same. Daniel's faithful testimony played a significant role in the king's newfound faith.

ᙡ First Impressions ᙡ

1. Why did Daniel's peers try to find fault with him? What does this reveal about their character? about their priorities?

2. Why were Daniel's enemies unable to find any fault? What sorts of things might they have been looking for? What does it reveal about Daniel that they found none?

3. How did Daniel's enemies come up with the idea of creating the new law? What does this reveal about Daniel's faith? about his public testimony?

4. *If you had been in Daniel's place, what would you have done upon hearing the new law? Why did Daniel go home and pray with his windows open?*

ᴗ Some Key Principles ᴗ

God's people should live above reproach.

The events of this chapter present a profound statement of Daniel's godly character. His political enemies were motivated by base envy, jealous of the favor the king showed to Daniel—favor that grew from his diligent service, in contrast to how Haman earned his great standing with King Ahasuerus. Those enemies were the most powerful men in the kingdom, and they set all their power and resources on finding something that Daniel had done wrong, some shortcoming or failure or character flaw with which to spoil his reputation—but they could find nothing!

Most people would cringe if they knew an enemy was trying diligently to discover something they had done wrong, something that would cause them embarrassment or shame if it were made known. Yet that is exactly what is happening for every believer, every day of the year! The enemy of our souls, the devil, is the accuser of all believers, and he works diligently, day and night, to bring accusations of sin against all who place their faith in Jesus Christ (Revelation 12:10). The devil's accusations are permanently silenced by the blood of Jesus Christ, for through His sacrifice we are found blameless before God. However, this does not give believers the license to indulge in sin. Quite the opposite, in fact.

Scripture calls God's people to live lives that are above reproach, so that the enemy cannot find a foothold or a source of accusation against us. As Paul wrote to the believers in Philippi, "Do all things without complaining and disputing, that you may become blameless and harmless, children of God without fault in the midst of a crooked and perverse generation, among whom you shine as lights in the world" (Philippians 2:14–15). Paul instructed Titus on the qualities required of elders and deacons, but those qualities should be the goal for every believer. "For a bishop must be blameless, as a steward of God, not self-willed, not quick-tempered, not given to wine, not violent, not greedy for money, but hospitable, a lover of what is good, sober-minded, just, holy, self-controlled, holding fast the faithful word as he has been taught, that he may be able, by sound doctrine, both to exhort and convict those who contradict" (Titus 1:7–9). When our lives are above reproach, we shine like beacons in a world of darkness.

There is only one God, and the only way to know Him is through His Son, Jesus Christ.

King Darius did not understand that there is only one true God; he was blinded by the teachings of the world, believing in some great pantheon of gods that supposedly ruled the created world. This ignorance made the king an easy prey for Daniel's enemies, who took advantage of it to deceive him into throwing his most loyal and valuable subject into the lions' den. Indeed, it was Darius's ignorance of God that led him to believe that he was himself a part of that fictitious pantheon of so-called gods.

This principle might seem self-evident to Christians, but the fact is that the world around us is completely ignorant of it. The world, in fact, hates this truth, because the world system is opposed to God's Word and to His Son, Jesus Christ. Virtually any religious system is tolerated and respected by the world—except the teachings of Jesus, which insist that He is the only source of salvation. One is free to teach openly about Islam, Buddhism, Hinduism, homemade New Age ideas, every form of paganism—but the one thing the world will not tolerate is the truth that there is only one God, and Jesus provides the only way to His presence.

Yet this truth is at the very core of Christianity. Jesus stated very clearly, "I am the way, the truth, and the life. No one comes to the Father except through Me" (John 14:6). There is no room for compromise on this truth, and there is no way that any other religious teaching can be melded in. Christianity is not compatible with any world religion, because it teaches that there is only one God and only one way to get to Him. As Paul reiterated, "For there is one God and one Mediator between God and men, the Man Christ Jesus, who gave Himself a ransom for all" (1 Timothy 2:5–6). Any other teaching is false.

Make prayer your first response to trouble.

Daniel was one of King Darius's most trusted counselors, and he probably had a large staff of assistants. When the king was considering the proclamation forbidding prayer to the Lord, Daniel could easily have raised a powerful protest. He might also have been aware of the real reason behind his enemies' plan to discredit him, and most men might have gone to the king to protest their innocence and expose the treachery. But Daniel did none of these things. When the king's edict was signed into law, he instead went home and knelt in private prayer.

The reason for this is that Daniel understood that only God could resolve the problem. He recognized that God's sovereign hand was involved, and that gave him the faith to turn it over to His control. In fact, it may well have been God's sovereignty and faithfulness that moved Daniel to give thanks (v. 10), turning a situation of fear into an occasion of thanksgiving. He knew the Lord was in control, and he rejoiced in the freedom of putting the outcome into His omnipotent hands.

Daniel might well have succumbed to anxiety and fear, wringing his hands in consternation over his predicament. But prayer is the solution to anxiety, because it is the process of taking the anxious burden to the Lord and letting Him take control. A thankful spirit is also an important element of prayer, since it grows out of the faith that He will answer our petitions. As Paul commanded, "Be anxious for nothing, but in everything by prayer and supplication, with thanksgiving, let your requests be made known to God; and the peace of God, which surpasses all understanding, will guard your hearts and minds through Christ Jesus" (Philippians 4:6–7).

Stand boldly for God.

It would have been fairly easy for Daniel to stay out of trouble after the king's edict was signed into law. After all, he didn't need to pray to Darius, and he didn't even need to stop praying to the Lord—just be discreet about it, that's all! A small change of habits—closing the windows in his upper room when he knelt in prayer, maybe not being so inflexible about how often he prayed, a little spirit of compromise—and everything would have been fine. No need to draw attention to yourself, no need to rock the boat; live and let live, and go with the flow.

But Daniel was not ashamed of his relationship with God, and he saw no need to hide behind closed doors as though his prayers were an embarrassing habit. He had always prayed with his windows open, evidently visible from the street below, and the threat of death in the lions' den did not deter him from continuing that practice. His refusal to honor the king's edict was not a belligerent flaunting of his faith; it was not an "in your face" gesture intended to provoke conflict. It was, however, a courageous refusal to hide his faith, because he was not ashamed to be counted as one of God's servants.

There are times when speaking openly of our faith in Christ requires courage, but we do well to imitate Daniel's example. This is not an excuse to use our faith as a weapon to browbeat others, but a call to not be ashamed of the gospel. Paul wrote,

"For I am not ashamed of the gospel of Christ, for it is the power of God to salvation for everyone who believes, for the Jew first and also for the Greek" (Romans 1:16). Yet he, too, asked his fellow believers to pray for him, "that I may open my mouth boldly to make known the mystery of the gospel, for which I am an ambassador in chains; that in it I may speak boldly, as I ought to speak" (Ephesians 6:19–20). The writer of Hebrews reminds us, "For He Himself has said, 'I will never leave you nor forsake you.' So we may boldly say: 'The Lord is my helper; I will not fear. What can man do to me?'" (Hebrews 13:5–6).

↜ DIGGING DEEPER ↝

5. *How did Daniel's testimony influence the people around him? What effect did it have in the king's life? on the nation as a whole?*

6. *What does it mean to live above reproach? How is this done? Give some practical examples of things that can bring reproach.*

7. *When have you stood up boldly for the gospel of Christ? When have you compromised to avoid confrontation? What resulted in each situation?*

8. In what ways does the world today reject the truth that Jesus is the only way to God? Why is this such an offense to the world? Why is it such an important doctrine of Christianity?

∿ Taking It Personally ∿

9. Have you come into a relationship with God through the salvation of Jesus Christ? If not, what is hindering you from doing so right now? If so, are you bold about your faith, or ashamed of it?

10. Make a list below of things you are thankful for. Each day this week, spend time in thanksgiving, adding to the list as other things come to mind.

DANIEL 7; REVELATION 13

⌁ THEMATIC BACKGROUND ⌁

We now return once more to the time of Belshazzar, king of Babylon, prior to the handwriting on the wall (Study 3). The Lord sent a dream to Daniel that bore some similarity to the dream of Nebuchadnezzar (Study 2), in that it addressed the Babylonian Empire and the kingdoms to follow. This time, however, the kingdoms were represented by strange beasts rather than by a huge statue; and this time the events described would extend far into the distant future—to times that have not yet come even today.

We will then zoom hundreds of years forward in time to join the apostle John on the island of Patmos, where he was exiled late in his life. Like Daniel, John was given a vision of the future, a vision that is reminiscent of Daniel's dream. In John's vision, however, we will learn more details about the things that are yet to come, and we will meet the terrible Antichrist and his false prophet.

The topic of end-times prophecy, or *eschatology*, is too large to address in detail in this one study, but these two chapters will give us an overview of God's plans for the future. More important, we will be reminded that God is sovereign over the future just as much as He has been in the past, and He will never forsake those whose names are written in the Book of Life. (For further study on this topic, see John MacArthur, *Because the Time is Near* [Moody Books, 2007].)

⌁ READING DANIEL 7:1–28 ⌁

FOUR BEASTS: *Daniel has a dream of his own that bears some similarities with the dream of Nebuchadnezzar (Study 2). This dream, however, goes farther into the future.*

1. THE FIRST YEAR OF BELSHAZZAR KING OF BABYLON: We now return to approximately 553 BC, fourteen years before the handwriting on the wall that we saw in

Study 3. The events in this chapter took place between Daniel chapters 4 and 5. The events portrayed in the dream, however, extend into the future.

2. THE GREAT SEA: The Mediterranean Sea.

3. FOUR GREAT BEASTS: These beasts represented the named kingdoms that we saw in Nebuchadnezzar's dream in Study 2—that is, Babylon, Medo-Persia, Greece, and Rome.

CAME UP FROM THE SEA: The ancient world frequently associated the sea with evil and dark mystery, and Scripture uses the sea to represent the realm of satanic activity (e.g., Isaiah 27:1). Something coming up out of the sea would immediately be suspicious in the minds of ancient people. This image will reappear in Revelation.

4. LIKE A LION, AND HAD EAGLE'S WINGS: The lion is the proverbial king of beasts, while the eagle is monarch of the skies. The mixed image suggested both the power and speed of the Babylonian Empire. Statues of winged lions actually stood outside the gates of the royal palaces of Babylon. Jeremiah (a contemporary of Daniel) similarly used both a lion and an eagle to picture Nebuchadnezzar (Jeremiah 49:19–22).

ITS WINGS WERE PLUCKED OFF: The remainder of this verse probably refers to the madness and healing of Nebuchadnezzar, which we considered in Study 7. His royal authority and humanity were plucked from him, but after he repented he was "lifted up from the earth" quite literally, as he stopped going about on all fours like an ox, and was "made to stand on two feet like a man." He was given a "man's heart" because he repented of his pride and humbled himself, thus reiterating the principle that pride debases a man but humility lifts him up.

WAS GIVEN TO IT: Notice that the text does not say, "It grew a man's heart," but that the man's heart was given to it. Throughout Daniel's visions, we will be reminded that God is the unseen controller of all events. It is He who raises up dominions, and He who throws them down.

5. A SECOND, LIKE A BEAR: The second beast is an image of Medo-Persia, which began its power as a co-rule of the Medes and Persians. The Persians soon surpassed the Medes, however, and the Medo-Persian Empire was "raised up on one side" to become the Persian Empire. The "three ribs in its mouth" represent the kingdoms defeated and absorbed ("between its teeth") by the Persian Empire: Babylon, Lydia, and Egypt. Bears were thought of as voracious devourers in ancient times, ponderous and always hungry.

THEY SAID THUS TO IT: The command to "devour much flesh" was fitting for the Persian Empire, which was the largest world rule up to its time. During the time of Esther, for example, Persia was attempting to absorb Greece, as we have seen previously. But more important here is the fact that we once again have an unseen Controller who is in charge of all events, the One who commanded Persia to expand, and who commanded it to diminish.

6. LIKE A LEOPARD: The leopard represents the Greek Empire under the leadership of Alexander the great. His conquest of the world was stunningly fast (he died at age thirty-three), which is pictured by the leopard's wings. The four heads probably represent the fact that the Greek Empire was split into four separate dominions after Alexander's death: Macedonia, Asia Minor, Syria, and Egypt. Leopards are known for their speed.

DOMINION WAS GIVEN TO IT: Once again, we find that God gave dominion to the leopard; it did not attain it under its own power.

THE FOURTH BEAST: *This beast is unnatural and hideous, unlike the preceding three. It also represents something not yet fulfilled in human history.*

7. DREADFUL AND TERRIBLE, EXCEEDINGLY STRONG: The fourth beast probably represents the Roman Empire. But notice the emphasis on its fearful aspect, underscored more emphatically than with the previous three beasts. The fact that this empire is not compared to any literal animal furthers this element of dread. Its huge iron teeth and nails of bronze (v. 19) that crush and rend and break in pieces, and its habit of trampling into the dust whatever it does not eat outright, suggest a wanton destructiveness. This kingdom was (and will be) characterized by brutality and lack of grace or beauty, something unnatural and contrary to the created order. Finally, note the downward progression in the animals pictured, from a lion and eagle to a bear to a leopard to a nightmare apparition. The world claims that mankind is evolving upward, but Scripture shows that we are degenerating downward.

TEN HORNS: Horns, like those of a bull, are used frequently in the prophetic Scriptures to represent world leaders. The Roman Empire fell apart in AD 476, yet its influence has continued to the present in the European states (and also in the political framework of the United States). The Empire will return to power around the second coming of Christ, under the authority of ten kings.

THE LITTLE HORN: *From the fourth beast there will arise a great world leader who will promise peace and prosperity. He turns out, however, to be Antichrist.*

8. ANOTHER HORN, A LITTLE ONE: This represents the rise of Antichrist, an individual human being ("eyes like the eyes of a man") who will speak boastfully and blasphemously (as we will see shortly).

106

9. THRONES WERE PUT IN PLACE: Daniel's vision now shifts dramatically, and he sees heaven preparing for the day of judgment. The Ancient of Days is the almighty God, seated in His holiness upon His throne of judgment, whose fiery wheels will consume the devil and his followers. The images of fire, emphasized with the interesting phrase "fiery flame," represent the all-consuming wrath of God that will one day burn away all sin and wickedness from the face of the earth.

10. TEN THOUSAND TIMES TEN THOUSAND STOOD BEFORE HIM: Every human who has ever lived will one day stand before God. Some will appear before His judgment seat, and some before the throne of grace. Where one stands after this life will be determined by how one responds to God in this life. God knows those who are His, and their names are written in "the books" that were opened here. We will see these books again in Revelation 13.

11. THE BEAST WAS SLAIN: The beast here refers to the fourth empire (probably Rome in its modern permutation), but also to Antichrist, whose blasphemies will be permitted for a season. His final destruction, which will occur at Christ's second coming, was also pictured by the stone in Nebuchadnezzar's dream that smashed the feet of clay (Study 2).

12. THE REST OF THE BEASTS: That is, the previous three beasts that represented earlier empires. Their "lives were prolonged" in the sense that each empire was absorbed into its successor, rather than utterly destroyed. As the Second Advent of Christ draws near, the modern descendants of all three empires will be part of the final phase of the Roman Empire, the fourth beast. Ultimately, however, all human government will be shattered and utterly destroyed, replaced by Christ's eternal kingdom.

THEY HAD THEIR DOMINION TAKEN AWAY: Yet again we are reminded that all earthly authority is bestowed by God, and He will also take it away. God is finally and completely sovereign over all events, both in heaven and on earth and under the earth.

THE SON OF MAN: *Daniel's dream is not all fear and horror; it culminates in the final triumph of Jesus Christ. But this triumph will include some suffering for the saints.*

13. ONE LIKE THE SON OF MAN: This is Jesus Christ, the Messiah, who often referred to Himself as "the Son of Man" (e.g., Matthew 16:27).

COMING WITH THE CLOUDS OF HEAVEN: Jesus will one day return to earth in bodily form to establish His kingdom (Revelation 20–22).

14. DOMINION AND GLORY AND A KINGDOM: Jesus Christ is King of kings and Lord of lords, eternal ruler of heaven and earth, and all authority has been given to Him by God the Father, the Ancient of Days. Peoples, nations, and languages are earthly distinctions, and this indicates that Christ will set up an earthly kingdom for a time, which will merge with His eternal kingdom. (See Revelation 20.)

15. THE VISIONS OF MY HEAD TROUBLED ME: Daniel may have been saddened to see that mankind would never improve his spiritual state, and the future would continue the cycles of sin and judgment.

17. FOUR KINGS: Probably the most notable ruler of each of the successive kingdoms: Nebuchadnezzar (Babylon), Cyrus (Persia), Alexander the Great (Greece), and the "little horn" or Antichrist. Anything that arises "out of the earth" is earthly and therefore corrupt and subject to death. The earth groans in longing for a kingdom that descends from heaven, which will be holy and righteous and eternal. That kingdom is coming!

18. THE SAINTS OF THE MOST HIGH: We will learn in Revelation that these are the people who have been saved by the blood of the Lamb, redeemed by Christ—that is, born-again Christians and God-fearing believers from all ages.

21. THE SAME HORN WAS MAKING WAR AGAINST THE SAINTS: God will permit the Antichrist to wage a great war against the saints, as we will see in Revelation 13, and he will even be allowed to prevail—for a season. But his wickedness will only further God's sovereign purposes, and when His plan is fulfilled, the wicked one shall be utterly undone.

22. THE TIME CAME FOR THE SAINTS TO POSSESS THE KINGDOM: Believers will enter the kingdom of Christ in its earthly phase following Jesus' second coming, having life that continues forever into the eternal state (Revelation 21–22).

23. DEVOUR THE WHOLE EARTH: The fourth and final human kingdom will be a worldwide order. The Lord showed Daniel that a unified world government will one day rule the earth (briefly), but it will actually "trample it and break it in pieces."

25. INTEND TO CHANGE TIMES AND LAW: The implications of this are not yet clear, but we have seen numerous times in these studies where kings have attempted to change God's law concerning worship. The rule of Antichrist will include laws prohibiting worship of the one true God and forcing worship of himself, making Darius's thirty-day prayer prohibition seem tame by comparison.

THE SAINTS SHALL BE GIVEN INTO HIS HAND: That is, God will permit Antichrist to persecute His saints for a time—but He will still hold absolute sovereignty over their affairs. God will allow His people to endure trial, but only under His sovereign control.

A TIME AND TIMES AND HALF A TIME: This refers to three and a half years, the last half of Antichrist's seven-year rule, continuing on to Christ's second coming.

26. THEY SHALL TAKE AWAY HIS DOMINION: The final rule of Antichrist will ultimately be no different from any other human kingdom, in the sense that God will permit its authority for a time, then revoke it. No power on earth or in heaven can stand against God's sovereign will.

27. HIS KINGDOM IS AN EVERLASTING KINGDOM: God's kingdom is entirely different from any earthly government, and it shall stand firm forever without end. What's more, all those redeemed by the blood of Christ shall participate in its rule!

ᔕ READING REVELATION 13:1–18 ᔐ

THE VISIONS OF APOSTLE JOHN: *We now move forward approximately six hundred years to the time following Jesus' resurrection. John's visions, however, carry us far into the future.*

1. THEN I STOOD ON THE SAND OF THE SEA: We now shift from the visions and dreams of Daniel to the visions of the apostle John during his exile on the island of Patmos near the end of his life.

A BEAST RISING UP OUT OF THE SEA: Here we have again the image of a beast rising from the sea, as we saw in Daniel's vision.

2. LEOPARD ... BEAR ... LION: Here we have the three natural beasts of Daniel's vision in reverse order. (Daniel listed them chronologically because he was looking forward in time, but John was looking backward.) The leopard represents Greece, the bear is Medo-Persia, and the lion is Babylon. This time, however, the traits of those animals are all combined into one beast, suggesting that this beast possesses the wicked elements of all human empires. Yet this beast represents more than generic tyranny; it represents one specific human being. This man will be the final earthly dictator, and he will stand violently opposed to the things of God. He is called Antichrist.

THE DRAGON GAVE HIM HIS POWER: Daniel's vision frequently reiterated the fact that the power and authority of the human governments was given by God, but this beast derives his power from the evil one. This does not, however, remove God from the picture. The devil can only empower Antichrist because God allows him to; the Almighty is still in charge.

3. HIS DEADLY WOUND WAS HEALED: This might refer to one of the kingdoms being destroyed, then revived, such as the Roman Empire. But it more likely foretells a fake death and resurrection hoax perpetrated by Antichrist as part of his lying deception (2 Thessalonians 2:9–10). In such a hoax, the evil one would be attempting to mimic the death and resurrection of Christ, setting himself on a par with the Son of God.

THE WORLD IS DECEIVED: *Antichrist and his false prophet will deceive the whole world into worshiping Satan. Those who refuse will suffer for it.*

ALL THE WORLD MARVELED: The world will be astounded and fascinated when Antichrist appears to rise from the dead. His charisma, brilliance, and attractive (though false) powers will cause the world to follow him unquestioningly.

4. THE DRAGON WHO GAVE AUTHORITY TO THE BEAST: That is, the devil, or Satan.

5. HE WAS GIVEN: Once again we are reminded that even the devil gains only the power that God gives him. The sovereign Lord of Creation will establish the limits within which Antichrist will be allowed to speak and operate. God will allow him to utter his blasphemies and deceive the world for three and a half years, or forty-two months. At the end of that time, the sovereign Lord will cast Satan and his minions into hell—and the devil will be powerless to resist.

7. MAKE WAR WITH THE SAINTS AND TO OVERCOME THEM: Several important things must be understood concerning this verse. First and foremost, note that it begins with the all-important clause "it was granted to him." God's saints will be persecuted and martyred during the time of great tribulation, but *God is still in control!* Second, the devil will overcome the saints *only on a physical, temporal level.* God's saints will never lose their salvation, nor will the Lord's controlling hand be hindered. They will lose their lives, property, and freedom, but nothing can separate them from the love and protection of God (Romans 8:38–39).

8. THE BOOK OF LIFE: This represents the names of every human being whom God has chosen to receive His free gift of salvation—chosen before "the foundation of the world," before time itself even existed. This eternal aspect of salvation demonstrates that nothing, not even Satan, can ever remove one's name from the Book of Life. "All who dwell on the earth" whose names are *not* written in that book will worship Antichrist.

11. ANOTHER BEAST: This is the final false prophet who promotes Antichrist's power and convinces the world to worship him as God. Antichrist will be primarily a political and military leader, but the false prophet will be a religious leader. Thus, politics and religion will ultimately unite in worship and allegiance to Antichrist.

110

TWO HORNS LIKE A LAMB AND SPOKE LIKE A DRAGON: Like Antichrist, the false prophet will put on an outward show of being godly, perhaps also claiming to be "a Christ." But his words will give away the lie, as he will speak on behalf of Satan, persuading the world to worship someone other than the one true God.

13. **PERFORMS GREAT SIGNS:** The false prophet will perform counterfeit miracles, attempting to claim for himself equal authority with Christ. Pharaoh's magicians did the same thing in Moses' time (Exodus 7). Elijah had called down fire from heaven to consume Baal's false prophets (1 Kings 18), and God will send two prophets during the end times who will do the same (Revelation 11:3–5). But God warned His people that they were to pay attention to a prophet's words more than to his signs and wonders; if he urges one to worship other gods, he is false regardless of his apparent power (Deuteronomy 13:1–5).

14. **WHICH HE WAS GRANTED TO DO:** And once again we are reminded that even the false prophet and Antichrist will have power only because God will grant it to them for a time. Without His permission, they could do nothing.

AN IMAGE TO THE BEAST: Like Nebuchadnezzar (Study 6), Antichrist will set up an image to himself, and the false prophet will persuade the world to bow in worship to it.

15. **GIVE BREATH TO THE IMAGE OF THE BEAST:** There is a subtle but important distinction here. The false prophet will give *breath* to the image, not *life*. (The Greek word *pneuma* used in this verse means "breath" or "spirit.") Antichrist will make his image appear to be alive through deceptive means.

16. **A MARK ON THEIR RIGHT HAND OR ON THEIR FOREHEADS:** Tattoos were used in ancient times to mark slaves and members of religious cults. Antichrist will similarly mark his followers in some identifying manner, and nobody will be permitted to buy or sell without it—making life nearly impossible for those who refuse to worship the devil's henchman. The exact nature of this mark is unknown as yet, but it will become clear as the time draws near.

18. **HIS NUMBER IS 666:** This is the essential number of a man. The number 6 falls one short of God's perfect number 7, and thus represents human imperfection. The threefold repetition of 6 underscores the fact that Antichrist, for all his power and apparent glory, will still be merely a man. The full meaning of this number and name is not yet apparent, but it, too, will be revealed in that day. "Let him who has understanding" be alert and discerning as that day draws near. God's people must be watchful for these signs, for the day of His appearing is close at hand.

∽ First Impressions ∾

1. Why do you think the prophecies were revealed through visions of animals, rather than direct and straightforward revelation? What emotional response does hearing about the animals create?

2. How would you describe the empire represented by Daniel's fourth beast? What characterized that empire in the past? What will characterize it in the future?

3. Which of the prophecies in these chapters have been fulfilled? Which have yet to be fulfilled?

4. How can a person distinguish between true prophecy and false prophecy?

↜ SOME KEY PRINCIPLES ↝

God is in complete control over the events of human history.

Throughout these studies, we have seen again and again that God is sovereign over the affairs of this world, from the smallest details to the most dramatic miracles. He caused a king to have insomnia one night; He kept three men unscathed inside the hottest furnace imaginable. He created all things with a word, He caused a virgin to give birth, His Son took on human flesh while still retaining His full godhood, then rose again from the dead—nothing is beyond His power, and all things work together according to His holy plan.

Yet we must not overlook the real-life circumstances through which He works out that plan. Some men faced death, going all the way inside that furnace or into that pit of lions; others faced hardship of every description with no guarantee that they would live through the day. We have seen empires rise and fall, kings and queens come and go. What's more, the future holds more of the same—and worse. We will see a worldwide empire rise to power that will outdo all other human governments for wickedness and abomination, and God's people will be called upon to suffer and be martyred.

Men and women have a tendency to see life through temporal eyes, focusing on the present hardship and dangers while missing the eternal glory that is to come. But God sees the struggles His people face—and sees far beyond them to the miraculous plans He is unfolding. God's sovereign hand controlled the events in Esther's life; He controlled the circumstances of Daniel's life; His plan was for the good of Daniel's friends as well as those around them; and His plan is for good in your life as well. He was sovereign at creation; He was sovereign throughout history; He is sovereign over the future; and He will remain sovereign for all eternity. Remember to remember this when hard times come!

Every person who has ever lived will one day stand before God, either for judgment or for eternal life.

"Then I saw a great white throne and Him who sat on it, from whose face the earth and the heaven fled away. And there was found no place for them. And I saw the dead, small and great, standing before God, and books were opened. And another book was opened, which is the Book of Life. And the dead were judged according to their works, by the things which were written in the books. The sea gave up the dead who were in it, and Death and Hades delivered up the dead who were in them. And they were judged, each one according to his works. Then Death and Hades were cast into the lake of fire. This is the second death. And anyone not found written in the Book of Life was cast into the lake of fire" (Revelation 20:11–15).

The Bible makes it very clear that a day of judgment is coming, and that every human being who has ever lived shall stand before God. However, *not all people will stand before God's great white throne of judgment.* The verses above describe the horrible throne of God's wrath, when those who are not written in the Book of Life shall be cast into the eternal lake of fire. Notice that these verses reiterate that "the dead were judged according to their works." This is not a good thing, although the world might think so. As Paul warns us, "For by grace you have been saved through faith, and that not of yourselves; it is the gift of God, not of works, lest anyone should boast" (Ephesians 2:8–9). To be judged according to one's works is to automatically face judgment, for without the saving grace of God, purchased by the blood of the Lamb (Jesus Christ), no person can gain the gift of eternal life.

There is only one way to escape the final, eternal judgment of God, and that is by having one's name written in the Book of Life. If you have repented of your sins and given your life to Jesus, your name is written in that book—and it can never be erased! But if you have not received God's gift of forgiveness, *available only through His Son, Jesus,* then you are at the most grave risk imaginable, in danger of eternal separation from God. The return of Christ is imminent, and the threat of judgment is real. But salvation is available to anyone who turns to God in faith. You have only hell to lose, and heaven to gain.

The devil deceives people away from God's truth.

A day is coming when a man will arise and deceive the entire world. He will persuade every nation on earth that he is God, probably claiming to be the reincarnation of Jesus or something along those lines. He will fake his own death and resurrection, and he will perform phony miracles—miracles that seem so real, they fool everybody. His powers of deception will be so great, so convincing, that the entire world will bow before him and worship him as God, and every person on earth will be branded with his number, indicating their allegiance to Antichrist.

But Christians must understand that this work of deception is not restricted to the end times or the Great Tribulation; it is going on right now, and has been since the beginning of the human race at creation. Satan has been a liar, the very father of lies, and a murderer since the beginning of time (John 8:44). He has worked diligently throughout human history, trying to deceive people away from God's truth, striving ruthlessly to bring souls into eternal condemnation along with himself. His great objective is to turn people away from the truth of Jesus Christ; he doesn't care who or what a person worships, so long as it is not Jesus. "Who is a liar," warns John, "but he who denies that Jesus is the Christ? He is antichrist who denies the Father and the Son" (1 John 2:22).

The devil is crafty, and his deceptions can seem very convincing. But there is ultimately one way to discern truth from lies: anyone who denies that Jesus is the only source of salvation is speaking a lie. John addressed this when he wrote, "By this you know the Spirit of God: Every spirit that confesses that Jesus Christ has come in the flesh is of God, and every spirit that does not confess that Jesus Christ has come in the flesh is not of God. And this is the spirit of the Antichrist, which you have heard was coming, and is now already in the world" (1 John 4:2–3). Jesus said, "I am the way, the truth, and the life. No one comes to the Father except through Me" (John 14:6). Those who reject Jesus also reject the truth; and those who reject truth by default embrace a lie.

↳ Digging Deeper ↲

5. *How will Antichrist be recognized? What will he be like? What will it be like for those under his earthly authority?*

6. *What trends do you see in earthly kingdoms as described in these visions? How does this compare with modern beliefs that mankind is evolving into something better?*

7. What events or trends in the world today indicate that the Lord's return is imminent? How does this imminence influence your life today?

8. What lies and deceptions is the devil using in the world today? How does he work to draw people away from the truth of Jesus Christ?

↳ Taking It Personally ↲

9. What evidences of God's sovereignty do you find in these chapters? How does His sovereignty influence your views of the future?

10. Do you trust the Lord of history with your own life? If not, turn from your sin and embrace the One who controls the events of the world.

Section 4:

Summary

Reviewing Key Principles

↶ Looking Back ↷

Over the course of these studies, we have witnessed God's people facing unexpected and dire circumstances. They were commanded to worship false idols, they faced annihilation at the hands of political enemies, and they were forced to interpret dreams that were not even described to them. They were threatened with death—in a fiery furnace, at the hungry jaws of lions, or by the swords of those who hated them. In every case, however, God's people stood firm in their obedience to His Word, and each time God proved that He is both sovereign and faithful.

We have also seen that God's sovereignty extends from before the foundation of the world, all the way into eternity. He is absolutely in control over all human events, and He is never caught by surprise. He works all things together for good for those who fear Him (Romans 8:28), and nothing can touch His people without His permission.

Below are a few of the major principles from the previous lessons. There are many more that we don't have room to reiterate, so take some time to review the earlier studies—or better still, to meditate upon the Scripture passages we have covered. Ask that the Holy Spirit give you wisdom and insight into His Word. He will not refuse.

↶ Some Key Principles ↷

God gives His people the words to speak at the right time.

Daniel found himself in numerous difficult situations, as we have already seen. He was called before several kings to interpret messages from God that no one else in the kingdom could comprehend—and at times his life was on the line. The Lord had given him the gift of interpreting dreams and prophecies, yet he made it abundantly clear that such interpretations were given to him directly from God; they were not the result of his own strength, wisdom, or abilities. And God was faithful in each instance to give Daniel the words he was to speak.

It's important to recognize, however, that Daniel did not know what he would say until the time came for him to speak. He did not know what words were written on the wall in Belshazzar's banquet hall until he got there, and he did not even know the content of Nebuchadnezzar's dream until the Lord revealed it to him. We can imagine how unnerving it must have been to have no idea what to say to a king demanding an interpretation where all others have failed. Yet this was precisely what the Lord called His servant to do, forcing Daniel to trust in God's faithfulness and sovereignty, and making it clear to the king and his court that the words were from Him.

This does not mean a Christian should be lazy and haphazard in the work the Lord calls him to do. Peter, for instance, urged his readers to "always be ready to give a defense to everyone who asks you a reason for the hope that is in you" (1 Peter 3:15). But Jesus also warned His disciples that they would sometimes "be brought before governors and kings" to give testimony to the gospel. At such times, the Lord said, "do not worry about how or what you should speak. For it will be given to you in that hour what you should speak; for it is not you who speak, but the Spirit of your Father who speaks in you" (Matthew 10:18–20). "I will give you a mouth and wisdom which all your adversaries will not be able to contradict or resist" (Luke 21:14–15). These verses are not an excuse for laziness but rather a comfort during persecution.

Just as God was faithful to give Daniel the right words at the right time, He will do the same for you. We can have confidence that God will enable us to be a faithful witness no matter the situation in which we find ourselves.

Worship the Creator, not His creation.

King Belshazzar threw a drunken party for his friends and courtiers, and in their licentious frenzy they ate and drank from sacred vessels that had been dedicated to the Lord's temple in Jerusalem. This blasphemous act demonstrated an utter contempt for the God of Israel, but the revelers took their blasphemy one step further: they openly praised and worshiped fictitious "gods of silver and gold, bronze and iron, wood and stone" (v. 23). In doing so, they worshiped the creation rather than the Creator.

Such paganism is still practiced today, and is in fact becoming very widespread in Western nations. Under the guise of "environmentalism," for example, many today deny that God created the earth and mankind, while simultaneously elevating His creation in His place. It is a bitter irony to treat the things of God with disdain, as Belshazzar did, while praising the very things He made.

The Bible warns that this idolatrous attitude inevitably leads to the downfall of a nation, just as it did in Babylon during the time of King Belshazzar. Paul wrote that the wonders of creation are intended to teach men about God, not to replace Him as their Lord. When a nation replaces the Creator with the creation, however, all forms of wickedness inevitably follow. "Professing to be wise," Paul warned, "they became fools, and changed the glory of the incorruptible God into an image made like corruptible man—and birds and four-footed animals and creeping things. Therefore God also gave them up to uncleanness, in the lusts of their hearts, to dishonor their bodies among themselves, who exchanged the truth of God for the lie, and worshiped and served the creature rather than the Creator, who is blessed forever" (Romans 1:22–25).

You might not learn the reason why.

It is tempting to focus on the honors and gifts Esther received when she entered the king's household, overlooking the hardship that must have been involved. She had been taken away from a godly home with no regard to her desires and was forced to live among women who had no knowledge of God or His commands. She spent at least a year in the women's quarters at the king's palace in an atmosphere that must have been highly charged with jealousy, envy, and competition. She had no idea who would be chosen as queen, and probably spent many sleepless nights wishing she could be back home with her cousin Mordecai.

Then one day, the Lord's plan was revealed to her—or at least part of it—when she was crowned as the king's new wife. Five years passed, during which she might well have assumed that she had come to a full understanding of the Lord's reason for taking her away from Mordecai's household. But the fullness of His plan had not yet been revealed, as she discovered after Haman hatched his diabolical plot. As Mordecai pointed out, "Who knows whether you have come to the kingdom for such a time as this?" (Esther 4:14). She did not come to understand the Lord's purposes until years had passed from the time of her hardship.

It is very encouraging when one can look back upon times of hardship and see how the Lord used the difficulties for His glory and our blessing; but we must also understand that the Lord does not always explain His reasons to us. Times of uncertainty and hardship require faith, a solid conviction that God is in control and is working out His perfect plan in our lives—even when we cannot understand what that plan is. The writer of Hebrews defines faith as "the substance of things hoped for, the evidence of things not seen" (Hebrews 11:1). The "hope" in this verse refers not to a wish that something might happen in the future but to a firm belief that God will keep His promises, working all things together for our good and His glory (Romans 8:28). We may not see what God's purpose is at present; indeed, we might not see His greatest purpose until eternity. But we can rest in the faith that His plan is being worked out, and the suffering will be nothing compared with the glory to be revealed. Our confidence is founded on His character.

Man's wrath does not produce God's righteousness.

It would appear that King Nebuchadnezzar's temper was modeled after his furnaces: fiery! His magicians asked to know what his dream was before offering an interpretation, and he roared, "If you do not make known the dream to me, and its interpretation, you shall be cut in pieces, and your houses shall be made an ash heap" (Daniel 2:5). His rage flared up instantly when his will was thwarted, and his punishments were extreme. Even after he realized that Daniel's friends served Almighty God, he resorted to his old threat of cutting in pieces any who spoke ill of God, making their houses as ash heaps.

The truth is that Nebuchadnezzar's anger was a natural consequence of his pride, not a righteous indignation against defiance or unlawful behavior. It was his pride that led him to create the golden image and command his nation to worship it, and that pride was offended when Daniel's friends refused to comply. His subsequent anger clouded his judgment, and he ended up defying the God of creation. If the king had humbled himself and cooled his anger, he might have recognized that the men's testimony was true and that his image was nothing more than a false god.

James warned his readers of the deadly trap of human wrath: "So then, my beloved brethren, let every man be swift to hear, slow to speak, slow to wrath; for the wrath of man does not produce the righteousness of God" (James 1:19–20). The Lord had raised up Daniel's friends as a witness to the king, offering him the chance to hear the truth concerning his idolatrous practices—but he refused to listen. Instead, he was quick to speak and quick to indulge his wrath, and as a result he quickly fell into deadly error. When anger flares up, take time to listen and pray. Quick speech can result in negative long-term consequences.

Pride debases a man, but humility lifts him up.

King Nebuchadnezzar was the most powerful man in the world, absolute sovereign over the Babylonian Empire. The world looked at him and saw a man who had enjoyed success in every venture, a man who had reached the pinnacle of human achievement. Then one day he suddenly went insane. His subjects watched aghast as he foraged through his royal garden, shuffling about on hands and knees, eating grass like a cow, his hair and nails grown filthy and unkempt, the rain and dew falling unheeded on his skin. How could such a great man be so suddenly debased?

But when God looked on Nebuchadnezzar, He did not see the pinnacle of humanity; He saw a man who had degraded his soul through pride and vanity. It was not a coincidence that the Lord chose to have the king go about on all fours; rather, He permitted the true nature of Nebuchadnezzar's pride to become evident to himself and the people around him. Pride is the sin of elevating oneself equal with God, and the paradoxical result is that it actually moves one *away* from God rather than toward Him. Mankind alone is made in the image of God, so any move away from God is also a move away from our intended human design—a move that makes us more like the beasts of the field.

"The fear of the LORD is to hate evil," wrote Solomon, describing God's perspective. "Pride and arrogance and the evil way and the perverse mouth I hate" (Proverbs 8:13). Proverbs 11:2 tells us, "A prideful spirit brings shame to a man, but humility brings wisdom." "Pride goes before destruction, and a haughty spirit before a fall" (Proverbs 16:18). Nebuchadnezzar had to learn the lesson that "A man's pride will bring him low, but the humble in spirit will retain honor" (Proverbs 29:23).

God's people should live above reproach.

The events of this chapter present a profound statement of Daniel's godly character. His political enemies were motivated by base envy, jealous of the favor the king showed to Daniel—favor that grew from his diligent service, in contrast to how Haman earned his great standing with King Ahasuerus. Those enemies were the most powerful men in the kingdom, and they set all their power and resources on finding something that Daniel had done wrong, some shortcoming or failure or character flaw with which to spoil his reputation—but they could find nothing!

Most people would cringe if they knew an enemy was trying diligently to discover something they had done wrong, something that would cause them embarrassment or shame if it were made known. Yet that is exactly what is happening for every believer, every day of the year! The enemy of our souls, the devil, is the accuser of all believers, and he works diligently, day and night, to bring accusations of sin against all who place their faith in Jesus Christ (Revelation 12:10). The devil's accusations are permanently silenced by the blood of Jesus Christ, for through His sacrifice we are found blameless before God. However, this does not give believers the license to indulge in sin. Quite the opposite, in fact.

Scripture calls God's people to live lives that are above reproach, so that the enemy cannot find a foothold or a source of accusation against us. Paul wrote to the believers in Philippi, "Do all things without complaining and disputing, that you may become blameless and harmless, children of God without fault in the midst of a crooked and perverse generation, among whom you shine as lights in the world" (Philippians 2:14–15). Paul instructed Titus on the qualities required of elders and deacons, but those qualities should be the goal for every believer. "For a bishop must be blameless, as a steward of God, not self-willed, not quick-tempered, not given to wine, not violent, not greedy for money, but hospitable, a lover of what is good, sober-minded, just, holy, self-controlled, holding fast the faithful word as he has been taught, that he may be able, by sound doctrine, both to exhort and convict those who contradict" (Titus 1:7–9). When our lives are above reproach, we shine like beacons in a world of darkness.

↶ Digging Deeper ↷

1. *What are some of the more important things you have learned from the books of Daniel and Esther? from Revelation?*

2. *Which of the concepts or principles have you found most encouraging? Which have been most challenging?*

3. *What aspects of "walking with God" are you already doing in your life? Which areas need strengthening?*

4. *Which of the characters we've studied have you felt the most drawn to? How might you emulate that person in your own life?*

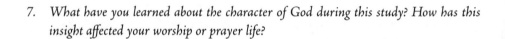

↶ Taking It Personally ↷

5. Have you taken a definite stand for Jesus Christ? Have you turned from your sin and believed the gospel? If not, what is preventing you?

6. What areas of your personal life have been most convicted during this study? What exact things will you do to address these convictions? Be specific.

7. What have you learned about the character of God during this study? How has this insight affected your worship or prayer life?

8. List below the specific things you want to see God do in your life in the coming month. List also the things you intend to change in your own life in that time. Return to this list in one month and hold yourself accountable to fulfill these things.

If you would like to continue in your study of the Old Testament, read the next title in this series, *Rebuilding God's City*, or the previous title, *Losing the Promised Land*.